THE ROMAN MIND

STUDIES IN THE HISTORY OF THOUGHT FROM CICERO TO MARCUS AURELIUS

by

M. L. CLARKE

*Professor of Latin in the University College of North Wales,
Bangor*

The Norton Library

W · W · NORTON & COMPANY · INC ·

NEW YORK

For permission to quote from copyright trans-
lations thanks are due to the following: Basil
Blackwell Ltd, for passages from C. J. Billson's
translation of the *Aeneid* and L. A. S. Jermyn's
translation of the *Georgics*; the Syndics of the
Cambridge University Press, for passages from
R. C. Trevelyan's translation of the *Georgics*;
Jonathan Cape Ltd, for passages from Cecil Day
Lewis's translation of the *Georgics*; Macmillan
& Co. Ltd, for a passage from the late Sir
Edward Marsh's translation of Horace's *Odes*;
and the Oxford University Press, for passages
from James Rhoades's translation of the *Aeneid*
and the *Eclogues*.

SBN   393   00452-X

CONTENTS

PREFACE

Historians of ancient thought seldom show much interest in the Romans. Their attention is directed to the Greek masters rather than to their Roman pupils. In the ancient world it was the Greeks who were the originators; the Romans did little more than reproduce Greek ideas in a different language and with at most a slightly different tone and accent, and it is not until St Augustine that we find a Latin-speaking thinker of undoubted originality, who has a place in the history of thought on his own merits. It is therefore understandable that the history of Roman thought should be neglected.

It would, however, be a mistake to ignore it or dismiss it as of minor importance. Its interest lies not so much in the originality or intrinsic value of the doctrines held as in the fact that particular men held them, and in the relation of the doctrines to the political and literary activities of their adherents. It has often happened in history that ideas have had as powerful an influence outside as within the country of their origin, and it might well be maintained that the Hellenistic philosophies exercised a more important influence in Rome than in the Greek world.

This book is not a complete history of Roman thought. I have not dealt in any detail with the ideas of the earlier Republic, nor have I attempted a full account of Roman religion, knowing that I had nothing to add to the admirable works of recognized authorities on this subject. I hope, however, that, incomplete though it is, the book will be of some use in introducing students of the classics to an aspect of ancient Rome which tends to be ignored in the standard histories of Rome and of Latin literature.

I have taken the opportunity of a second impression to make a few corrections and minor alterations.

February 1960   M. L. C.

INTRODUCTION

THE DEVELOPMENT of Roman culture is closely linked with the history of Rome's expansion. As Polybius observed, no people was more ready than the Romans to adopt the customs of others and to imitate what was superior in them.[1] As she expanded from a small city state to become the mistress first of Italy, then of a world-wide empire, Rome took over and assimilated the material civilization, the literary forms and the ideas of the peoples she conquered.

By far the most important influence, indeed the only important one in the intellectual sphere, was that of Greece. Greek civilization had spread far beyond the mainland of Greece; it extended throughout the Eastern Mediterranean, and touched Italy itself in the Greek cities of the south. It was from these cities that Greek influences first came to Rome. Latin literature begins with a Greek from south Italy, Livius Andronicus, and in the latter part of the third century B.C., when Rome was still engaged in the struggle with Carthage and before she had turned eastwards, tragedies and comedies based on the Greek were already being performed at Rome. Then in the second century came Rome's rapid expansion in the East, and with it a first-hand acquaintance with the main centres of Greek civilization and an influx of Greek teachers and men of learning into Rome. The Romans as ever were ready pupils; conquered Greece provided men of letters, philosophers and experts in the various arts and sciences to enrich the life of her conquerors.

Greek influence on Rome is often thought of as something transmitted through books and expressed in literary imitation. It was more than this. Greek civilization was something living and pervasive, whose influence it was impossible to escape. In every branch of learning the Greeks had expert knowledge, teaching experience and systematic textbooks; they taught in their own language and, conscious of the superiority of their culture, saw no reason to modify their teaching for the benefit of the barbarians of Italy who were their latest pupils. The Romans, who had no philosophy or science of their own, and only a rudimentary literature, had no choice but to learn from the Greeks. It would hardly have been surprising if Rome had become completely absorbed by the civilization of the Greek world and scarcely distinguishable in the sphere of culture from the Hellenistic kingdoms. That this did not happen must be attributed, in part at any rate, to Rome's geographical position. She stood just outside the range of Hellenistic civilization and sufficiently far from its nearest centres to be able to develop and consolidate her own language and way of life, so that when she came into close contact with the Greeks she was able to absorb their culture without losing her own distinctive qualities.

Of the Roman way of life and thought before the influx of Greek ideas it is hard to speak with any certainty, for Rome only developed a literature late in her history and as a result of Greek influence, and little reliance can be placed on reconstructions of Rome's early days such as that of Livy. A consciousness of the loss of old traditions led to a regretful looking back to the past and the establishment of a legend of the virtues of *maiores nostri* which can hardly be accepted as historical. But though no doubt there was more of peasant tenacity than of pure virtue in the old Romans, it is easy to believe that in early days Rome could rely on a patriotism and spirit of disinterested service that her citizens hardly showed in later ages; for such a spirit is naturally fostered by the existence of hostile powers threatening the state and as naturally fades when, as happened to Rome after the defeat of Carthage, the state finds itself without serious enemies.

There survived into imperial times the memory of the old discipline by which the youth of Rome had been trained. It was a matter of tradition imbibed in the home and the camp and the forum. The mother brought up her son in his early years, the father taught him until he put on the *toga virilis*, after which he was initiated into public life either by his father or by some respected person acting in the place of a parent.[2] The mother would pass on the traditional morality of the home, the father would teach his son letters and other useful knowledge; in the camp and the forum the young man would learn by example and experience the arts of war and politics.

This old Roman education was based on a threefold foundation: the family, the state and religion. The family was all-important. At its head was the *pater familias,* exercising an absolute authority over his children and dominating the household. From him the child would imbibe that loyalty to family tradition which was one of the strongest elements in the formation of the Roman character. He would learn of the great deeds of his ancestors and grow up anxious to emulate them:

> *virtutes generis mieis moribus accumulavi;*
> *progeniem genui, facta patris petiei.*
> *maiorum optenui laudem, ut sibi me esse creatum*
> *laetentur; stirpem nobilitavit honor.*[*3]

So runs one of the epitaphs of the Scipio's. The repeated emphasis on family tradition needs no comment. The spirit which the epitaph expresses finds confirmation in the words of the young Scipio Aemilianus, a member by adoption of the same family, quoted by Polybius, the Greek historian who was deported to Rome after the battle of Pydna in 168 B.C. and remained there to become the admirer of Rome and the friend of Scipio. Scipio, Polybius tells us, was uneasily conscious that some people thought him an unworthy representative of his family; when Polybius attempted to reassure him and offered his help, Scipio eagerly accepted the offer, assuring the Greek that once accepted by him as a friend he would think himself worthy of his family and his ancestors.[4]

It is Polybius, too, who bears witness to the impression which would be made on a Roman boy by the bizarre ceremony which took place at the funeral of an eminent Roman, when the masks of his distinguished ancestors were brought out and worn by actors marching in procession and impersonating the ancestors. 'It would not be easy', says Polybius, 'to provide a fairer spectacle for an ambitious and generous boy. Who would not be moved to see the representations of men famous for their valour

---

* By my conduct I added to the virtues of my family; I begat offspring and sought to equal the deeds of my father. I maintained the glory of my ancestors, so that they rejoice that I was their offspring; my honours have ennobled my stock.

grouped together as if alive?'[5] Best of all, Polybius goes on, the young are stimulated to bear every kind of hardship for the common good, hoping thereby to gain the glory which is given to brave men. The family merges into the state. The way to gain glory for the family was by serving the state in war and peace. And service to the state was learned through the same discipline and obedience and respect for tradition that operated in the home. 'It was the ancient custom,' writes Pliny, 'that we should learn from our elders not only by hearing but also by seeing what we should ourselves in due course do and then hand down in turn to our successors. Thus the young were early taught by service in the camp so that they should learn to command by obeying, to be leaders by following; thus too when entering on a political career they stood at the doors of the senate house and watched the conduct of public business before they took part in it. Each had his father for master or if he had no father, a man of distinction and ripe age took the father's place.'[6] The state was a kind of extension of the household. As the son of a farmer learned the traditional lore of the countryside from his father and grew up ambitious to maintain and extend the family estate, so the young man learned the arts of war and politics by a kind of apprenticeship and hoped to maintain the political community to which he belonged, extend its bounds and pass it on to the next generation.

Closely bound up with both the family and the state was religion. The boy at home would observe and take part in the various ritual acts prescribed by tradition; in public life he might well hold one of the state priesthoods and would at any rate be well acquainted with those religious spectacles whose number and splendour so impressed Polybius.[7] Thus he would imbibe as part of the tradition in which he was brought up a feeling of reverence for the gods and a sense that the well-being of the state was bound up with the due performance of their rites.

Roman religion produced no teachers or prophets. It remained an affair of cult and ritual, supported by tradition and sentiment and unable to develop on its own or to assimilate from outside either theology or moral teaching. Yet those who grew up to its practice would be insensibly influenced by it. Its close connection with the various processes of life in the home, the farm and the state would foster a sense of tradition and social solidarity, and its orderliness and insistence on the correct manner of proceeding, its conception of man's relations with the gods as something in the nature of a legal contract, would encourage a similar attitude in man's relations with his fellow-men. One of the most striking passages in Polybius's account of Roman institutions is that in which he contrasts the unreliability of the Greeks in money matters with the honesty of the Romans; and this honesty he attributes to the influence of religion.[8]

Such then in brief was the traditional Roman discipline. The second century B.C. saw the advent of professional teachers from Greece to supplement or supplant the old methods of upbringing. We have two accounts of the education of the children of distinguished Romans of this period which give a clear picture of the contrast between old and new ways. The old tradition is represented by Cato the Censor, who made himself personally responsible for the education of his son, taught him reading, law and Roman history, and trained him in throwing the javelin, fighting in armour and riding, and in boxing and swimming. The new methods are exemplified in the education which Aemilius Paulus gave to his children; though he passed on to them the traditional Roman training he had himself received, he was more concerned to give them a thorough Greek education. He employed a variety of teachers, grammarians, philosophers, rhetoricians, teachers of sculpture and drawing and experts on hunting, and all of them Greeks.[9] Paulus's methods prevailed over Cato's; the Greek type of education, intellectual in content and conducted by professionals, expert in their respective subjects, became established at Rome and the old training in the home became little more than a memory.

Among the Greek teachers who were now to be found not only as private tutors in the households of distinguished Romans like Aemilius Paulus but also teaching publicly were philosophers, and they brought with them ideas that were new and strange and, in the eyes of conservative Romans, dangerous. Thus we find sporadic attempts on the part of the Roman authorities to keep them out. We hear of the expulsion of two Epicureans in 173 B.C., and a decree expelling philosophers (along with rhetoricians) was passed in 161.[10] But such actions had no permanent effect; the philosophers were soon back again. On one occasion they had the pretext of an official mission. In 155 B.C. the Athenians sent an embassy to Rome consisting of their three leading philosophers, Critolaus the Peripatetic, Diogenes the Stoic and Carneades the Academic. As it took some time to settle the official business of the embassy, the philosophers took the opportunity to give some lectures. These caused a sensation; the young Romans flocked to hear them, with, according to Plutarch, the general approval of their elders. It was left to Cato, the champion of Roman traditions against Greek influences, to sense danger. He did his best to get the Roman authorities to make up their minds, so that the Greeks could get out of Rome as quickly as possible.[11] But the harm, from Cato's point of view, was done; from now on Romans could not escape the influence of Greek philosophy.

Carneades, the most distinguished of the three philosophers, was famous as a destructive critic, and when in his lectures at Rome he chose justice as his subject and argued first on one side then on the other, refuting on the second day the defence of justice which he had offered on the previous day, it is not surprising that he met with some disapproval. There were, however, among the Greeks grave responsible moralists as well as clever destructive critics, and Greek philosophy was to prove not so much an unsettling influence as a source which could supply something to take the place of decaying Roman traditions. The sudden increase in wealth and responsibilities which came with Rome's eastward expansion brought with it new temptations, and some Romans no doubt learned only new vices and luxuries from their association with the Greeks. But there were also those who learned different lessons. The friendship of Scipio Aemilianus with Polybius to which we have already referred provides the best illustration of the way in which the Romans now looked to the Greeks for guidance. Polybius describes how the friendship originated with the loan of some books. The two began to see a good deal of one another, and one day, when Scipio, a young man of eighteen, was walking along with Polybius, he asked in an embarrassed manner why Polybius always spoke to his brother and not to himself; was it because he thought him a mild and useless sort of person, unworthy of the traditions of his family? Polybius assured him that he had no intention of ignoring him, and did his best to restore his self-confidence. He pointed out that there were plenty of learned Greeks who could help him in his studies, and offered his own help and support to Scipio in his more personal difficulties. Scipio warmly accepted the offer, and from that time the two lived in the closest intimacy. Polybius goes on to describe how Scipio set himself a high standard of conduct, avoiding both the laxness in sexual morality and the avariciousness in money matters shown by many of his contemporaries.[12]

The learned Greeks to whom Polybius referred included masters of the various arts and sciences, men of letters, scholars and rhetoricians, and all these helped to form the new Roman culture. But what was most significant was the new influence exercised by philosophy on men's conduct. It was no longer enough to guide one's life by inherited tradition; Romans now turned to the rational morality of Greek philosophy, and in particular to that system which seemed most in harmony with Roman tradition, Stoicism. In the century which followed the embassy of the three philosophers Greek philosophy became firmly established at Rome, and in the age of Cicero a well educated Roman was expected to have some philosophical knowledge, while there were not a few on whom such studies had more than a superficial influence. The extent to which philosophy succeeded in permeating Roman life can be seen by a comparison between Cato the Censor and his great-grandson, Cicero's contemporary, Cato of Utica. The elder Cato had fought a stubborn battle against Greek influences, and, as we have seen, had done his best to get the philosophers out of Rome in 155 B.C. The younger Cato was conscious of no such conflict between Roman traditions and Greek ideas; while cherishing the memory of his ancestor and remaining a thorough Roman, he was yet the outstanding example of a life guided by the precepts of Greek philosophy.

I

THE BACKGROUND OF THOUGHT
IN THE CICERONIAN AGE

THE TRADITIONAL Roman upbringing which we have described in the Introduction had by Cicero's day become almost a thing of the past. Parental influence had waned, and the average father was probably content to leave his sons in the hands of slaves and professional teachers and himself to take only a rather distant interest in their progress. Cicero himself had a series of Greek tutors for his son, and when he himself took a hand in his education it was not to inculcate a traditional Roman morality but to help the boy along with what one might call his school work. The two literary works which Cicero addressed to his son, *Partitiones Oratoriae* and *De Officiis*, were concerned with rhetoric and philosophy respectively, that is to say, with the two disciplines which constituted the higher education introduced from Greece.

The Roman tradition of family life cannot have counted for much in the urban emancipated society of late-republican Rome, with its political marriages and easy divorces and its large households of slaves. Nor did Roman religion mean much to homes which had lost touch with the life of the countryside in which that religion had its roots. What force it retained was due to its connections with patriotic sentiment. It still had a hold on the Roman's emotions. It had little hold on his intellect, for his intellect was trained by Greek philosophers who had little or no sympathy with Roman sentiment.

In public life the old tradition still had some life. The Romans did not learn the arts of politics and war from the Greeks; Greek political theory might be studied by a few, and some might even read Greek writings on military science,[1] but such influences were of small importance compared to the

Roman tradition handed down in the forum, the senate house and the camp. In political life the system of apprenticeship was still to some extent in operation. Cicero was entrusted by his father to Scaevola, committed his sayings to memory and tried to profit by his wisdom and experience, and he himself guided the young Caelius on his first entry into public life.[2] But the old spirit had by then been lost. Caelius and his contemporaries were hardly dutiful obedient pupils anxious to follow in the footsteps of their ancestors, learning to lead by learning to obey.

There is evidence too that the familiarity with Roman traditions which had been acquired naturally and easily as a result of the traditional Roman education was becoming a thing of the past. Boys of Cicero's generation were made to learn by heart the old Roman code of laws, the Twelve Tables, but the practice fell into disuse; 'no one now learns them', wrote Cicero towards the end of his life.[3] Orators in the law courts often showed themselves sadly ignorant of the law, and Cicero was moved to protest against the neglect of a study which was not only useful but delightful, and which was indeed a patriotic duty.[4] As Cicero said elsewhere, the Romans were like foreigners in their own city.[5]

The professional teachers from whom the Romans learned were either Greeks or, if not Greeks, were strongly influenced by Greek educational tradition. The regular education of the young Roman was normally confined to literature and rhetoric, the art of the *grammaticus* and the art of the *rhetor*. Some attempt had been made by the Latin *grammatici* to provide a literature course based on the old Roman poets; when Horace was at school under Orbilius in the middle of the first century B.C. he was made to read the works of Livius Andronicus. But it was not until after Virgil had been adopted as a school text that Latin literature had its place equal to Greek in Roman education; before then it was on Greek literature that the Roman was mainly nourished. Rhetoric was taught in Latin by the time of Cicero's youth, but the substance of it was entirely Greek, and even small details show its Greek origin. We read for instance with some surprise in a Latin rhetorical treatise of the first century B.C. that mankind is to be divided according to nationality into two classes, Greeks and barbarians.[6] Such was the prestige of the Greeks intellectually that the Romans who adapted their textbooks felt no need or desire to remove such incongruities.

The rhetoricians did not claim to do more than teach the art of speaking. They might commend their subject by enlarging on the civilizing influence of oratory and the benefits to society which resulted from its use, but they soon left such topics and got down to the technical details of the construction of a speech, the topics of argument and the adornments of style. There was, however, a section in which they touched on wider matters. When dealing with deliberative oratory and its aims they took the opportunity to define some moral concepts. For the deliberative orator concerns himself with the good and must therefore know what it is. The good, so the Roman learned from his rhetoric master, comprises the four virtues of wisdom, justice, courage and continence. In justice were included a number of virtues and duties, such as compassion for the innocent and suppliants, gratitude to the deserving, the punishment of those who have done ill, the keeping of faith, the observance of the laws of society, of friendship, of the family and of religion.[7] We get the impression of a mixture of Greek traditional morality and philosophy. There is some Stoic influence in the definitions of the virtues, but the section as a whole does not bear the stamp of any single school of philosophy. Cicero in his *De Inventione*, which may be taken as reflecting accurately the views of the rhetorical teachers under whom he sat in his youth, while holding that virtues are good in themselves, finds place for the opposing view that they are commended by their utility. There are, he says, three classes of desirable things: those which attract us for their own sake, those which are desirable on account of the advantages they bring and those in which the two elements are combined; and even justice, the most important of the virtues, is found to have a certain element of expediency about it. It originates in nature; but there are some things which become customary as a result of their usefulness, and what springs from nature and is approved by custom is supported by religion and law.[8] Thus the opposing principles represented in contemporary philosophy by Stoicism and Epicureanism are skilfully combined.

On the whole the rhetoricians were on the side of the angels. Teachers tend to moralize, and the examples used by the rhetorical teachers show that they took the opportunity to instil into their pupils some sound morality. 'The man who holds nothing sweeter than life cannot live a virtuous life.' 'Riches are not to be compared with virtue.' 'Account that man free who is slave to no wickedness.' 'The man who can never be satisfied is no less in want than he who has not enough.' 'The good life consists entirely in virtue, since virtue alone is in one's own power and everything else in the power of fortune.' 'The wise man will meet every danger on behalf of the state.' Such were the adages which the rhetorician handed out to his pupils and which in some cases were made the subject of school exercises.[9] Rhetoric, which in the days of the sophists had been subversive of morality, with its claim to make the worse cause appear the better, had for so long been in the hands of the schoolmasters that it had become almost respectable. We experience some surprise when we read a sentence in *Ad Herennium*: 'Craft is displayed in bribery, in promises, dissimulation, surprise, lying and other matters which I shall handle on a more appropriate occasion if ever I write on warfare and politics.'[10] The proposed treatise, which might have provided an interesting antidote to the prevailing Roman self-righteousness, was unfortunately never written, and we are left with a mere hint of a cynical outlook which contrasts with the academic classifications and trite morality which the rhetorician contributed to the Roman's training in public life. On the other hand, there always remained a non-moral element in rhetoric; the pupil was taught to argue on both sides of a case and to depreciate virtue as well as to commend it.

We have attempted to show what the Roman of the late Republic acquired from his upbringing and education. We now turn to the speeches of Cicero to see what light they throw on contemporary opinion. We should remember that these speeches provide no such body of evidence as that provided by the Attic orators for fourth-century Athens, since we have extant from

Rome only the speeches of one man, and that a man of exceptional gifts. We should remember too that Cicero generally has a point to prove, and the views he expresses may be in part adopted in order to reinforce the case he is pleading. None the less it is unlikely that in addressing the senate or the people or the judges in the courts he would have said anything which would not commend itself to his audience, and his speeches provide the best evidence we have for the accepted views of his day. Bearing in mind, therefore, the limitations of the evidence we may use the speeches in an attempt to reconstruct the outlook of the ordinary Roman in the period from 81 B.C. when Cicero made his first speech, to his death in 43 B.C.

First let us consider religion. The theme is common enough in the speeches, and the impression we get is that religious belief is firmly established. How, says Cicero, can one deny the existence of the gods when one observes the manifest signs of design in nature? Heaven and earth and sea are guided by Jupiter; from him come the goods of life, the light we enjoy, the air we breathe. The gods hear men's utterances and know their thoughts. At times they may wink at men's crimes; yet they lend their help to the good and punish the wicked. Nothing should be asked of them but what is good and just; true piety consists in a right view of the divine power.[11]

The best teacher of religious observance is the Roman tradition; the writings of the philosophers on the nature of divinity are all very well, but one might well suppose them to be derived from the wisdom of the old Romans. Rome has surpassed all peoples and nations in piety and religion and in that wisdom which consists in recognizing that all things are guided and governed by the divine power.[12] It is the gods who have guided and preserved Rome and given her her Empire. Who could deny that the city of Rome above all things is directed by the power of the gods? It is they rather than human reason that counsel and govern the state; they saved Rome from the threat of Catiline and inspired and guided Cicero in the defeat of the conspiracy.[13]

It is indeed generally in connection with patriotic sentiment that Cicero makes use of the appeal to religion; speaking in the heart of Rome, under the shadow of the Capitol, with signs of Roman power and greatness about him, it was easy and natural for him to think in terms not of rational theology but of the old city state patriotism; the heavens declare the glory of God, but no less does the greatness of Roman power.[14] It is the gods of the city of Rome, Jupiter, Juno and Minerva, the Penates and Vesta to whom Cicero generally appeals.[15] When Catiline threatened the state the gods themselves, not at a distance, but present in Rome, defended their temples and the buildings of the city; Jupiter himself resisted the conspirators' attack.[16]

In addition to religious feeling we find that family loyalty and patriotism are assumed to be binding on Cicero's listeners. We should hold our parents to be dearest of all, because we receive from them life, patrimony, freedom and citizenship. Nature binds one to one's parents and offspring, and *pietas*—a word which in Cicero's speeches generally refers to one's duty towards one's parents—is the foundation of all virtues.[17] So too with one's country: the fatherland is the common parent of us all, than which nothing can be dearer or sweeter.[18]

This is not the place for a study of Cicero's political outlook as shown in his speeches; this belongs to history, and can only be studied in relation to the particular situation with which each speech deals. We can, however, note some of the political themes which recur in the speeches and which seem to be part of the common stock of Roman ideas. Most striking perhaps is the belief in tradition. Progress, reform, improvement find no place among Cicero's political ideals; *novae res* in Roman political terminology is equivalent to revolution, and Cicero couples 'those desirous of new things' (*novarum rerum cupidi*) with 'disturbers of the peace' (*turbulenti homines*) as men who must be guarded against if the Roman state is to survive.[19] To the younger generation Cicero's message is that they should follow the example of their forefathers and preserve the constitution so wisely drawn up by them.[20]

The belief in tradition includes a belief in the political ideals peculiar to Rome. The historian who looks back on the age of Cicero with the knowledge of later developments thinks of the Roman Republic as on the point of death, as a 'mere name', in

the phrase attributed to Julius Caesar.²¹ Yet for all its weakness
the Republic had created a tradition of thought and sentiment
to which the orator could confidently appeal. This is shown by
Cicero's frequent references to freedom (*libertas*) and his assumption that this freedom was a part of the Roman tradition.²² It
was not forgotten that Rome had once been ruled by kings and
that their removal had marked the foundation of Roman
liberty and the end of absolutism.²³ In defending one of his
clients Cicero found it necessary to apologize for his having
entered into the service of a king, where obedience and subjection to the will of another are obligatory; it is, he admits,
the height of folly to enter into a position where one must lose
one's freedom.²⁴ Freedom is something that has been won and
handed down with much toil from past generations to the
present, and in the enjoyment of which Rome surpasses all
other states.²⁵ The possession of freedom is, like the outward
appearance of Rome, the light men look upon, and the soil of
their fatherland, a source of affection and delight to all. All
other nations can endure slavery; Rome cannot, simply because
other peoples avoid toil and pain and are ready to suffer anything to be free from them, whereas the Romans are brought
up by ancestral tradition to refer all thoughts and acts to honour
and virtue.²⁶

We do not expect to find a detailed analysis of political concepts in oratory, and often no doubt it would be idle to enquire
too closely what Cicero meant by *libertas*. He does, however, in
one place tell us that the essence of a free state is that neither
the life nor the goods of a citizen can be touched without a
decision of the senate or the people or whatever body has the
constitutional right to make the decision,²⁶ and this perhaps is
the essential feature, or at any rate an important feature, of the
Roman idea of freedom. To the Greeks freedom meant an equal
sharing of the management of the affairs of the city; for the
Romans it was rather the enjoyment by the individual of certain
rights.

One of the commonest themes in the speeches and one which
we may suppose was drawn from the common stock of contemporary ideas is the decline of Cicero's own age from the high

standards of the past. The old Romans, according to Cicero, cultivated their fields and did not covet those of others, and in this way they raised Rome from insignificance to a great Empire.[27] In their own private life they lived simply, content with the minimum, while in public life they considered only the splendour and glory of the state.[28] They were virtuous, frugal, hardy, grave and austere; they spurned all pleasures and lived a life of physical and mental energy, desiring nothing but what conduced to glory and honour.[29] Faithful to their obligations, they regarded carelessness in the execution of a commission as no less a disgrace than dishonesty.[30] They executed the law fairly and strictly.[31] They excelled in political wisdom, foreseeing all contingencies and laying down rules even for the smallest matters.[32] In home affairs office was then open to worth rather than noble birth; in relations with other states the Romans were mild and lenient. Dependents and allies they defended from aggression; even their enemies were well treated and after defeat often had their possessions restored to them.[33] As Cicero looks back on the past he is moved to exclaim that the old Romans deserve to be revered and worshipped as divine.[34]

Such is the picture of the past which Cicero's speeches give us; the present offers a sad contrast. The austere virtues of the ancients have long since disappeared. Honesty in the courts is a thing of the past; the state is sick almost to death.[35] The present age looks with envy on merit. The old political discipline is slipping away; the old leniency has given birth to cruelty and inhumanity.[36]

In general we observe that politics are approached from a moral standpoint. In a candidate for office, says Cicero, goodness, uprightness and integrity are generally required rather than fluency of speech or expert knowledge. Roman magistrates are like bailiffs of an estate: if they have some skill, so much the better, if not, those who chose them are content with moral worth and blamelessness.[37] In the same way in the matter of provincial government it is the moral character of the governors, their rapacity or disinterestedness that Cicero emphasizes. He exposes, when it suits him, the crimes of Rome and the unpopularity of her rule, but he thinks of the problem as a moral one. If the old virtues could be restored, all would be well. Men rather than measures are needed.

What are the virtues which the Romans particularly admired? Firstly there is *virtus* itself. The word is often used in the speeches, and generally with a suggestion of stern and manly qualities; the ideal is the strong minded, self-controlled man who can despise all pleasures and spend his life in bodily and mental exertion.[38] The word *virtus* is sometimes joined with *constantia* and *gravitas*, those qualities on which the Roman so prided himself; associated with these is *magnitudo animi*, that lofty spirit which never yields to fortune or circumstances.[39] Loyalty, trustworthiness, integrity, frugality and self-control complete the picture of the virtuous Roman.[40] But besides the austerer virtues there are milder and softer qualities which are recognized as having a place in human character, qualities such as pity, clemency, humanity and kindness. Greatness of spirit needed the admixture of some kind-heartedness to be acceptable; clemency and mildness are said to win general admiration.[41] Marcellus's *misericordia* is recalled as well as his *virtus* and *fides*; Scipio Africanus is remembered for his championship of the distressed.[42] *Mansuetudo* is a virtue of Pompey; Catulus is praised for his *humanitas*, Caesar for his *clementia*.[43] Cicero himself liked to claim that he was by nature mild and prone to pity and had been forced to assume a severe character only for reasons of state.[44]

Nor does Cicero ignore the claims of friendship. It is described as a sacred bond and the chief source of pleasure in life.[45] Its object is utilitarian (the purpose of friendship, says Cicero, is the regulation of the good of all by mutual service[46]), but it is also based on community of feeling, for 'there is no surer bond of friendship than agreement and unity of aims and wishes'.[47]

It is by helping others, says Cicero on one occasion, that man approaches closest to divinity.[48] Normally, however, he does not call in religion to support morality.[49] Nor does he accept any mythological supports to morality. We are not to suppose, he says, that the wicked are pursued by furies; man's own bad conscience plays the part of the furies.[50] Nor do we find Cicero appealing to the idea of rewards and punishments after death. There is, he says, quoting the views of the philosophers, either no life after death, or a higher life of the spirit freed from the body.[51] When he speaks in his own person it is rather the immortality of fame that he stresses.[52] Cicero himself had, so he claims, after his return from exile, won a kind of immortality, since the memory of the senate's benefits to him would never die.[53] Those who die for their country, he claims, do not suffer death, but rather attain immortality.[54] The life of the dead depends on the memory of the living; the greatest reward man can gain is glory, which 'alone offers the memory of mankind as consolation for the brevity of life, ensures that though absent we are present, though dead we live' and provides 'the ladder by which men climb to heaven'.[55]

Cicero liked to maintain that his oratory was founded in philosophy and that his speeches were full of philosophic maxims,[56] but one would not expect an orator engaged in the day-to-day business of politics and litigation to reproduce in his speeches much of his private philosophical studies, and in truth it is seldom that we come across in them any remarks that bear an unmistakable stamp of philosophic influence. When Cicero, addressing Caesar in *Pro Marcello*, claims that generosity and wisdom are not only the highest but the sole goods, one is reminded of Stoic doctrine, and when in the *Philippics* he lays down that law is nothing but right reason derived from the divine power, commending good action and forbidding bad, the influence of Stoicism is patent.[57] But normally when he refers to distinctive philosophic tenets he either rejects them, as in the case of Epicureanism, and of Cato's Stoicism as caricatured in *Pro Murena*, or he respectfully declines to commit himself.[58] The maxims of the speeches derive not so much from Cicero's own studies in philosophy as from the conventional copybook morality of the rhetorical schools. In one of his speeches we read: 'It must be that avarice arises from luxury: from avarice springs desperate daring; and from this source come all crimes and evil doing.'[59] The idea and the manner of expression are closely paralleled in one of the examples quoted in the rhetorical treatise *Ad Herennium*: 'Folly gives rise to inordinate desires. These give birth to avarice, and avarice drives men to every sort of evil doing.'[60] The speech from which the quotation is taken is an early one, composed when Cicero was still fairly fresh from the schools. But even in one of his mature speeches, *Pro Sestio*, we find an eloquent passage on patriotism which turns out on investigation to be based on what was evidently one of the stock themes of the rhetorical schools.[61]

From what has been said of the ideas expressed in Cicero's speeches it will be seen that they provide no evidence that Epicureanism had spread sufficiently to become part of the accepted ideas of the day. There were certainly not a few Epicureans among Cicero's contemporaries, but their views remained those of a minority and could safely be ignored, or assumed to be unacceptable. So far as the speeches of Cicero show any philosophical influence it is that of Stoicism, a philosophy whose ideas had become widely diffused and could be assimilated without great difficulty to the Roman tradition. It will be noted too that the prevailing tone of the speeches is a moral one. In the Athens of the fifth century political oratory might be completely divorced from morality; Thucydides has recorded how in the debate on the fate of Mytilene the vindictiveness of Cleon was opposed not by appeals to the moral sense but by hard-headed realism. Such was not the spirit of the Roman curia and forum. Open Machiavellianism was not a feature of public life at Rome; whatever dubious methods the orator might use to win his case, whatever the intrigues to which he might sink in the struggle for power, he was careful to profess high motives and appeal to worthy sentiments.

Finally, we must remark here on a point on which more will be said later. The atmosphere of the speeches is noticeably different from that of Cicero's philosophical works. In the latter the spirit is the Greek one of disinterested inquiry; in the former it is the Roman one of sentiment and love of tradition. Thus in the matter of religion the treatises *De Natura Deorum* and *De Divinatione* are rationalist and sceptical, whereas the speeches give the impression that the strength of religion is unimpaired. The Greek atmosphere which prevailed in the study had not spread to the forum.

II

EPICUREANISM

RHETORIC AND PHILOSOPHY were the two main intellectual disciplines of the Greek world, and teachers of both were active in Rome. But the task of the philosophers was not quite so easy nor was their position quite the same as that of the rhetoricians. The latter found a people used to public speaking and ready, once the initial prejudice had been overcome, to learn from those who professed to teach it. The philosophers, on the other hand, had to overcome not only the general prejudice against foreign teachers, but also the Roman unfamiliarity with, and lack of interest in, intellectual inquiry. Rhetoric naturally led to a career, at the bar and in politics, and thus became part of the established educational system. Philosophy was more of a private and personal matter, an intellectual interest to engage the Roman in his leisure moments, or a support to his moral convictions and a comfort in his distress; it remained, so far as education was concerned, an 'extra', something which the educated man might study or not according to his choice. Moreover, whereas rhetoric was taught according to a system on which there was no fundamental disagreement, in philosophy there were a number of different doctrines competing for allegiance.

By the first century the old opposition to philosophy had died down and philosophers were free to come and go as they wished. There was freedom to learn as well as to teach; one could take one's choice and adhere to which school one liked. Cicero observed with disapproval that many of his contemporaries, following some friend or carried away by the first lecture they heard, attached themselves to one of the dogmatic schools at an age when they were incapable of judging the issues and before hearing all sides of the case.[1] But this was not for lack of teachers to put the different points of view. Cicero himself studied under teachers of the Epicurean, Stoic and Academic schools and welcomed the freedom of his age, believing that philosophy flourished on disagreement.[2]

There were four established schools of philosophy, centred in Athens, each with its recognized head: the Academy, the Peripatetic school, the Stoic and the Epicurean. The two older schools were the least influential. The Peripatetics were scholarly and sensible, but made little impression on the world. The Academy had been introduced to Rome in the person of Carneades, a brilliant destructive critic, who made a sensation by his agile debating when he visited Rome as one of the envoys of 155 B.C.; but, though it had a distinguished advocate in Cicero, its apparent lack of any positive doctrine prevented it from having much influence at Rome.[3] More important were the two characteristic philosophies of the Hellenistic age, Stoicism and Epicureanism. Unlike the older schools they were dogmatic and had a positive message to mankind. They were the missionary schools, carrying out propaganda and trying to convert, and it was they that competed for the allegiance of the Romans in the last years of the Republic.

Of the two Epicureanism presented the sharper challenge to traditional Roman ideas. Its utilitarian ethics undermined the accepted ideal of Roman virtue, and its picture of the gods as remote powerless beings existing in the perfect peace of inactivity in the regions between the worlds was inconsistent with the traditional religion of Rome. Epicureanism had no use for family sentiment or the ideal of public service; its founder advised against marriage and parenthood, recommended abstention from politics and advised his followers to live unobtrusively. Moreover, the Epicureans cared little for literary culture and the graces of style, and they expected their adherents to acquire peace of mind by studying physics, whereas the average Roman valued style and literary culture and had little interest in the nature of the physical world.

In spite of all this Epicureanism made considerable headway, and for a time in the last years of the Republic it had a numerous following, perhaps more numerous than that of the Stoics.

Cicero's works give us the names of a number of Roman Epicureans, and the influence of the school was evidently not confined to his circle. 'They carry the people with them', says Cicero.[4] They were the first in the field with philosophical treatises in Latin, poorly written according to Cicero, but presumably easily understood by the ordinary man. Amafinius, the earliest of these Epicurean writers, was followed by others, and, to quote Cicero again, 'they won over the whole of Italy'.[5]

If we are to believe Cicero, the Epicureans had won a spectacular success. Why was this? Cicero himself suggests three reasons: their philosophy was easy, its doctrine of pleasure as the sole good was attractive and, as there was nothing better available, men took what they could get.[6] The second reason was the obvious one for a hostile critic to suggest, but if any Roman believed Epicurus to be an advocate of sensual enjoyment, his knowledge of his master's teaching was extremely superficial. Cicero himself knew well enough that Epicurus's interpretation of pleasure had led him to something like an austere asceticism. One Roman Epicurean at least, as we know from his own words, believed that virtue belonged to Epicureanism no less than to Stoicism. Cassius writing to Cicero explains that it is difficult to persuade men that the good is desirable for its own sake; but that virtue produces pleasure and peace of mind is both true and easily proved. He quotes Epicurus's words that a life of pleasure is impossible without a life of goodness and justice, and concludes by saying that the so-called 'lovers of pleasure are in reality lovers of the good and of justice.'[7]

There was no doubt some truth in Cicero's suggestion that the spread of Epicureanism was due to the ease with which it could be understood, for Epicurus and his followers had the art of popularizing, and could reduce their system to a few simple propositions. Cicero's third reason, that the Romans took what they could get because there was nothing better available, emphasizes the weakness of the Roman tradition, and its inability to provide an adequate guide to life. This weakness had already shown itself in the second century B.C. when Scipio Aemilianus had turned to Greeks like Panaetius and Polybius for

support, but whereas then it was the Stoics who provided guidance, it seems that when Cicero wrote they had failed to maintain
their position. Their Roman followers may have been too intent
on cultivating their own moral character to spread their doctrines
among their countrymen; they certainly neglected the written
word. The field was left open to the Epicureans, who provided
an explanation of the universe which was at any rate complete
and consistent, and could satisfy the intellect if not the
emotions, and which had the strength of a dogmatic system
handed down from a revered master and faithfully maintained
by a united community of believers. The system was open to
criticism at certain points, and it was criticized, but the Roman
Epicurean knew that there was an answer to the criticisms. If
he could not give the answer himself he could always refer the
matter, like Torquatus in *De Finibus*, to his Greek masters.[3]

To the Epicurean Epicurus was the deliverer of mankind
from the fear of death and of divine intervention. Mankind,
according to Lucretius, was crushed by the weight of religion,
oppressed by the fear of death and of the life after death.
Epicurus in his day had challenged the power of religion, but
the task had not been completed, and Lucretius is evidently
convinced that his master's message is as relevant to the Rome
of his day as to the Athens of Epicurus.

If the Romans of Lucretius's day were really oppressed under
the burden of religion and obsessed with dark fears, Epicureanism may well have come as a welcome release, and there is no
need to look for further reasons for its appeal. But this is not
the impression we get from Cicero. 'I am often surprised', he
writes in the *Tusculans,* 'at the presumption of some philosophers who extol the knowledge of nature, and offer exultant
thanks to the discoverer and founder of this knowledge and
venerate him as a god. They say that by him they have been
freed from the tyranny of constant fear and terror by day and
night. What fear? What terror? Is there any old woman so mad
as to be frightened of all those things which I suppose you
would fear if you had not learned natural science?'—by the
traditional picture, that is, of the underworld, a picture which
Cicero elsewhere dismisses as a monstrous invention of poets

and painters which no one in his senses would believe.[9] To this it may be answered that Cicero represents only the opinion of the educated minority, and had little knowledge of the outlook of the common people. But, though this may be granted, we remain without evidence of any widespread fear of divine wrath or punishment after death. Such ideas hardly occur at all in traditional Roman religion. Rome had no mythology of the life after death; the picture of the underworld with its grim figures of Charon and Cerberus, its gloomy rivers, its judges and its punishments, came from Greece, and came in the main through literature.

This mythology no doubt made some impression on the Romans, but it cannot have gone very deep, and it would certainly not be true to say that it dominated men's minds in the last years of the Republic.[10] Fears and superstitions there no doubt were in the Rome of Lucretius's day, and to some the study of nature as explained by Epicurus may have brought a sense of freedom and emancipation. But in all ages men who feel that they have a message to their fellowmen tend to exaggerate the miseries from which their message brings release. Lucretius, convinced that fear of the gods and fear of death are the root of all evil, exaggerates the extent to which his contemporaries were dominated by these fears.

One more point may be suggested in explanation of the spread of Epicureanism. It should be remembered that its popularity at Rome did not outlast the end of the Republic, and any attempt to explain its success in Cicero's day should also take into account its failure in the generation that followed. To some extent, perhaps, it was an intellectual fashion which passed as fashions do. But it may be that it satisfied a real human need which was peculiar to the late Roman Republic. Philosophies, or religions, owe their appeal in part to the fact that they supply something which the society of the day does not. Epicurus's teaching offered peace. The strife, unrest and self-seeking of the Roman world in the last years of the Republic led men by way of reaction to the quiet atmosphere of the Garden. The community of friends living quietly and without ambition had a special attraction against a background of civil

war and restless ambitions. At first sight it may seem strange
that a quietist philosophy that grew from the decay of the
Athenian city state should make an appeal to the vigorous,
politically minded Romans; but perhaps its appeal was not so
much in spite of, as because of, those qualities which were alien
to the Roman tradition.

We must now look closer at Epicureanism and see what its
message involved. What would Memmius, or any other reader,
have found when he started to read the *De Rerum Natura*?
After the invocation of Venus he would read how a man of
Greece first dared to raise his eyes and stand up against religion,
broke forth like a victorious general, traversed the whole boundless universe, and returned in triumph with the knowledge of
the truth about nature. But though Epicurus had won the
victory, the work still had to be done. Men were still ignorant
of the causes of things and resorted to supernatural explanations. Their mental darkness must be scattered not by the rays
of the sun, but by the knowledge of nature.

We have already said something of Lucretius's diagnosis. As
for his prescription, it suggests that Epicureanism was not quite
so easy as Cicero liked to make out. The explanation of nature
was fundamental to Epicureanism, and it is this that forms the
substance of Lucretius's six long books. It was knowledge that
Epicurus brought back from beyond the *flammantia moenia
mundi,* knowledge of what can be and what cannot. It was
enough for the Stoic to 'wrap himself up in his own virtue'; the
Epicurean had to 'know the causes of things'. Epicureanism
was, it is true, dogmatic, and its adherents were not encouraged
to speculate on their own; yet it did answer all the questions,
and it preserved something of the old Greek spirit of rational
thought, although fossilized in a dogmatic system. Whether
true or false, scientific or unscientific, it had in it something
which Rome could ill afford to lose.

But it is legitimate to doubt whether physical theory was as
attractive to other Romans as it was to Lucretius. Most readers
of *De Rerum Natura* would probably have been more interested
by what its author had to say on mankind and human conduct.
On the all important question of the *summum bonum* they

would have found that Lucretius had little to say; that was not his subject. But they would have found a striking passage in the fifth book, in which man is placed in the context of the physical world, and the origin of his species and of the civilization he has created is traced.

Man, according to Lucretius's account, had no divine origin; he was not created by or born from the gods. The first men came out of the earth, which was in a quite literal sense 'mother earth' and, like a human mother, eventually ceased bearing. In early days men were much hardier than now; at first they lived like beasts, feeding on what earth provided, without fire, living in woods and caves, without any law or society, each taking what he could get. Then men began to build huts, learned the use of fire and took to marriage. They joined together in society, for the sake of self-protection. The earliest societies were monarchical, ruled by men of outstanding ability. These distributed flocks and fields at first to the strong and good-looking; later, with the invention of property and gold, wealth was honoured rather than physical qualities. The kings were overthrown; disorder and violence followed, but this led to the establishment of laws and constitutional government. The arts and crafts, the use of metals, agriculture, etc., were discovered by the imitation of the processes of nature. All these things were gradually improved as a result of practice. 'Practice and the inventiveness of the tireless mind taught them little by little as they went forward step by step.'[11]

Lucretius's picture of the origin and growth of civilization is in marked contrast to the old idea of the Golden Age followed by decline. But it would be a mistake to suppose that at that time there was any general belief in the Golden Age. We must rid our minds of the impression given by the Augustan poets, who make so much of this myth. In Lucretius's day it was known as a poetic fiction, not to be taken seriously.[12] The commonly accepted view was that man had originally lived much like the beasts. In the introduction to Cicero's *De Inventione* we read that there was once a time when men wandered about in the fields like animals, relying not on reason but on physical strength. There was no knowledge of religion

or human duties, no marriage or law. Men were scattered in the
fields or hidden in lairs in the woods until some great and wise
man transformed them from wild savages to a mild and gentle
way of life.[13] Such was the view of the rhetorical teachers whom
Cicero followed. The great and wise man to whom they
attributed the work of civilization was of course an orator. The
philosophers preferred to call him a philosopher, but they too
accepted the idea that civilized life had replaced a primitive
and beast-like existence.[14] Thus there was nothing novel about
the general idea of a change from barbarity to civilization.

On the other hand, the picture of man's rise given by
Lucretius differs from what we have seen to be the accepted
view of his day, not only in the detail in which it is worked
out, but in the importance assigned to the development of the
arts and crafts, the emphasis on learning by experience, and
the fact that the agency of the great man is dispensed with. The
whole passage, if not as novel as is commonly supposed, was
certainly striking. Yet one can hardly say that Lucretius's
views on the origin of society had any great influence on his
attitude to man. One might perhaps have expected that the
spectacle of man's rise from lowly origins to an advanced
civilization by his own unaided efforts would have led to an
enthusiastic confidence in man and a belief in further advances
to come. Lucretius, however, finds little encouragement in the
spectacle. He points out that in spite of the dangers of primitive
life deaths were not so very much more frequent then than
now; men were no doubt killed by wild beasts, but there were
no slaughters of vast numbers in war or by shipwreck; some
then died of hunger, but nowadays men ruin themselves by
over-eating.[15] What we have at the time, he points out, seems
best until something better is discovered. In old days skins
were so valued that men quarrelled and fought for them; now
it is gold and purple that cause the trouble, and 'the greater
fault lies with us', because we can do without our luxuries,
whereas primitive man could not do without his necessities.
'So the race of man toils fruitlessly and in vain for ever, and
wastes its life in idle cares, because, we may be sure, it has not
learnt what are the limits of possession and how far true

pleasure can increase.'[16] For Epicurus true pleasure can easily be found by the satisfaction of simple wants; luxuries bring no increase of pleasure, and once man has acquired technical skill sufficient to satisfy these wants there is no need for any further advance.

Though in one place Lucretius allows the possibility of further progress in some arts,[17] elsewhere he seems to suggest that man has gone as far as he can go, when he ends his account of the growth of civilization with the words: 'They saw one thing after another grow clear in their minds until by their arts they reached the highest pinnacle.'[18] So Epicurus, he tells us, had found mankind adequately supplied for their material needs; what was wrong was the human heart.[19] Lucretius's account of the origin of civilization, brilliant as it is, does not open up any new prospects for mankind. The achievements of man were irrelevant; what was important was the right attitude of mind.

The aim and end of life, according to Epicurus, was pleasure, and 'by pleasure we mean the absence of pain in the body and trouble in the soul. It is not a succession of drinking feasts and of revelry, not sexual love, not the enjoyment of fish and other delicacies of a luxurious table that produce a pleasant life; it is sober reasoning, searching out the grounds of every choice and avoidance and banishing mere opinions, which cause the greatest tumults to take possession of the soul.'[20] Such was Epicurus's interpretation of pleasure. On the other hand he could not, and did not, deny that bodily pleasures were pleasures, and he left a remark which caused some embarrassment to his followers, that he could not conceive of pleasure other than the pleasures of the palate, of sex, and of sight and hearing.[21] His opponents pressed him with the inconsistency; he seemed at once to be preaching asceticism and self-indulgence.[22] But even if his theory was inconsistent, his own practice and precept were clear enough, and his followers gave little ground for complaint to the most severe moralist. 'Pleasure', exclaims the Epicurean spokesman in *De Finibus*, 'so far from being a matter of voluptuous and effeminate self-indulgence, is austere, self-controlled, severe.'[23] The function of Epicureanism was to free man not only from fears, but also from desires. Desires were insatiable, and from them arose hatred, schism, disunion, civil strife and war.[24] Like the moralists of the opposing school, the Epicureans saw desires, or at any rate excessive desires, as diseases of the mind.[25]

As regards the pleasures of the table, Epicurean teaching was clear enough. 'Plain food', says Epicurus, 'brings no less pleasure than costly diet once the pain of want has been removed, and bread and water give the highest possible pleasure when they are brought to hungry lips.'[26] Men's bodily needs can be easily supplied, and pleasure can result from the simple life. Lucretius, after painting a picture of a luxurious banquet in a rich palace, contrasts with it that of men lying on the grass by a stream of water under the branches of a tall tree, refreshing their bodies at no great cost.[27]

As regards the pleasures of sex Epicurus left behind a number of discouraging remarks. 'The wise man will not fall in love.' 'Sexual intercourse never did anyone any good; and he will be lucky if it did not actually do harm.' 'Love is a strong yearning for sexual pleasure accompanied by goading and restlessness.'[28] Like so many other things, love involved too many pains to qualify as pleasure. Some Epicureans, it seems, were not quite satisfied with this negative position and followed out a line of thought suggested by Epicurus himself when he divided desires into the natural and necessary, the natural and unnecessary, and the unnatural and unnecessary. Desires in the second category, among which was counted sexual desire, were, according to Epicurus, not difficult to satisfy; his followers accordingly held the pleasures of sex to be 'easy, common to all and ready to hand'.[29] Thus there was some ground in Epicurean theory for regarding sexual desire as something which was to be satisfied in the easiest way, without being taken too seriously; Philodemus, who was evidently no ascetic, and Horace in his early days when he was under Epicurean influence, took this line.[30]

Lucretius's attitude is rather different. He too recommends a resort to *Venus Vulgivaga*, but for him love is not a pleasure, but rather a *dira cupido* which must be prevented from getting the upper hand. The violence of his attack on the passion of love suggests that to him, at any rate, it was a more potent disturber of peace of mind than it had been to the passionless Epicurus. Lucretius is in general accord with his master's attitude, but his sharp and painful consciousness of the force of this desire brings him close to the moralists of a different tradition who, seeing in love only an irrational disturbance of the soul, included prescriptions for avoiding it in their *medicina animi*.[31] Even the Cynics, in other respects so far from the Epicureans, would in this respect have recognized Lucretius as a kindred spirit.[32]

Another desire which the Epicureans saw as an enemy of peace of mind was the desire for power and glory.[33] Lucretius dissociates himself from the struggles and ambitions of contemporary politics. 'Nothing', he writes, 'is more gladdening than to dwell in the calm regions, firmly embattled on the heights by the teaching of the wise, whence you can look down on others and see them wandering hither and thither, going astray as they seek the way of life, in strife matching their wits or rival claims of birth, struggling night and day by surpassing effort to rise up to the height of power and gain possession of the world.'[34] Elsewhere he returns to the same theme, pointing to the dangers and troubles which attend ambition and the envy which the great incur. 'Wherefore let them sweat out their life blood, worn away to no purpose, battling their way along the narrow path of ambition; inasmuch as their wisdom is but from the lips of others, and they seek things rather through hearsay than from their own feelings.' 'It is far better', he holds, 'to obey in peace than to long to rule the world and to sway kingdoms.'[35]

Thus we see that in many ways Epicurean moralizing approached that of the Stoics. The theoretical difference remained; the argument and polemics continued. But the attitude to life was fundamentally the same. Stoics and Epicureans alike condemned avarice, ambition, luxury and desires of various kinds. When one reads Lucretius's lines about the restless noble rushing from place to place but never escaping from his own boredom, one might, so far as the theme goes, be listening to Seneca preaching on the Stoic text of *constantia*.[36] Even Cicero

when he writes as a moralist in the *Tusculans* is quite ready
to forget polemics and hold up Epicurus as an example of a
philosopher free from desires and fears, armed against all the
ills of life.[37] The Epicureans in fact shared that attitude to life
which found so ready an acceptance in the Greek world after
its confidence in man's powers had been shaken by Alexander's
conquests, an attitude of retreat from the world, limitation of
desires and cultivation of independence of circumstances, an
attitude which the Romans, for all their mastery of the world,
seemed unable to resist.

We have seen how Epicurean teaching involved a denial of
many of the commonly accepted goods of life. Love, marriage
and family life, political activity, literature and the arts, everything indeed that the humanist values, meant nothing to the
Epicurean. He was left only with friendship and science. In
friendship he had indeed something which sweetened life,
but science did not appeal to everybody, and was moreover
presented by the Epicureans in a narrow and uninspiring form.
They showed no desire to set it up as a worthier intellectual
activity than literary study and to establish a new scientific
culture to replace the accepted παιδεία of the day. The Epicurean
in *De Finibus*, in answer to criticisms of Epicurus's lack of
culture, can only claim that the art of living which he studied
was of more use than the arts he rejected.[38]

The Roman Epicureans were not, however, all consistent
followers of their master. Even their Greek teachers did not
always conform to the pattern set by Epicurus. Philodemus
with his elegant epigrams and his works of literary criticism
was a cultured man of the world as well as a tireless contro-
versialist; Phaedrus could be described by his old pupil Cicero
as 'polished and humane'.[39] Lucretius himself was a poet and
proud of his ability to touch all things with the charm of the
muses; even if he had purged himself of all political ambitions,
his philosophy did not prevent him from seeking fame through
poetry.[40] Lesser men like Torquatus did not allow themselves
to be deterred by Epicurus from literary pursuits.[41] In particular,
Epicurus's advice to avoid politics seems to have sat lightly on
the Roman Epicureans. Atticus, it is true, remained behind the

scenes, imperturbable and indispensable, keeping on good terms with all parties, and at least providing an illustration of the practical advantages of ἀταραξία. But others were not prepared to stand aside; Lucretius's advice to 'obey in peace' was not likely to meet with a favourable response from one brought up in the tradition of the Roman governing class. Titus Albucius, the 'complete Epicurean', as Cicero calls him, suffered exile as a result of disobeying his master's command to avoid politics.[42] Torquatus, bearer of a name famous in Roman history, followed the traditions of his class rather than the precepts of Epicurus, held the praetorship, and fought and died on the Pompeian side in the civil war. Cassius too refused to 'obey in peace'; his conversion to Epicureanism did not result in his retirement from politics; it did not prevent him from leading the forces of republicanism and proving himself, in the words of Cremutius Cordus, 'the last of the Romans'.[43]

III

STOICISM

POPULAR THOUGH Epicureanism was in the time of Cicero, if we consider Roman history as a whole we must conclude that the most influential philosophy among the Romans was Stoicism. Even in Republican times, though the actual number of Roman Stoics may have been comparatively small, the influence of the school was more widely diffused than that of Epicureanism and was felt outside the ranks of its professed adherents. It was less rigid and more adaptable than Epicureanism; it was susceptible of various interpretations, and within its ranks could be found men of personality and originality like Panaetius and Posidonius. It was on better terms than were the Epicureans with other philosophies, especially in the first century B.C. when the Academy under Antiochus abandoned the critical attitude of Carneades and came to the conclusion that there was very little real difference between Plato and Zeno.

The Stoics were also less sharply divided than the Epicureans from popular non-philosophic thought. They found a place for the gods of traditional religion by a process of allegorizing, and they accepted divination. They proved by reason a number of things that the average Roman believed by instinct, such as that it was natural to love one's children and right to take part in public life, and they put forward an ideal of virtuous conduct which chimed in well enough with the traditions of duty and self-sacrifice handed down from *maiores nostri*. If the virtues of *gravitas, constantia* and *magnitudo animi* were really, as Cicero considered, peculiarly Roman, it might even be said that the early Romans had been Stoics before they ever heard of Stoicism, for these virtues were certainly among those that made up the Stoic ideal of conduct.

On the other hand, there were alien and unsympathetic

features in Stoicism. The Stoics, at any rate the founders of the school, Chrysippus in particular, were tedious, unattractive writers with a taste for uncouth technical terms and relentless logic-chopping, and a man of taste might well revolt from them. Their moral teaching too was in some ways repellent; they framed their doctrine in the form of paradoxes contrary to common sense and common feeling. They set up the impossible figure of the ideal wise man free from all emotions and branded all others as fools and madmen; they held that the commonly accepted goods of the world were of no account, that there was a great gulf fixed between virtue and vice, and that all who did not attain to virtue were equally bad. Cicero, when he wished to discredit Cato in his speech for Murena, could easily make out his Stoicism to be an inhuman fantastic creed:

> The wise man is never moved by favour, never pardons anyone's faults; only the foolish and weak-minded show pity; it is unmanly to allow yourself to be persuaded by prayers and services; only the wise are beautiful—however deformed they may be; they alone are rich—even if utter beggars; kings—even if in a state of slavery. And we who are not wise men are runaways, exiles, enemies, madmen. All wrong actions are equal; every misdeed is a foul crime, and it is as bad to strangle a cock unnecessarily as to strangle your father. The wise man never holds an opinion, never repents, is never mistaken, never changes his mind.[1]

Yet this very rigidity was a source of strength. Adaptable though Stoicism might be, there remained the hard core of idealism, the uncompromising message of Zeno that virtue was the sole good. And this would impress even the critical and unsympathetic. Cicero, genial and tolerant, viewing philosophy from the sceptical intellectual standpoint of the Academic school, was none the less tempted at times to take the view that the Stoics were the only philosophers.[2]

The influence of Stoicism at Rome began to be felt in the middle of the second century B.C. Polybius assured Scipio Aemilianus that he would find plenty of people to help him in his studies among the educated Greeks who were flocking to

Rome at that time.³ Among these Greeks was the Stoic Panaetius, who first came to Rome about 144 and became Scipio's friend and guide. Tiberius Gracchus had a Stoic philosopher, Blossius of Cumae, as counsellor, and in the period round the end of the second century and the beginning of the first we know of a number of eminent Romans, Q. Aelius Tubero, Q. Mucius Scaevola, C. Fannius, P. Rutilius Rufus and others, who followed the Stoic creed. One of these at any rate provided a model of a life lived in accordance with Stoic precepts. Rutilius Rufus was noted for the blamelessness of his private life and his honesty in public life. His disinterested conduct in Asia made him so unpopular with the tax farmers and the equestrian order generally that on his return they engineered his trial and condemnation. He spent the rest of his life in exile, bearing his lot with philosophic calm, and left behind him the memory of a blameless man unjustly condemned, a confessor, if not one of the martyrs, of Stoicism.

In the age of Cicero Stoicism was not so strongly represented. It had, however, one outstanding adherent in Cato the younger, who lived and died in accordance with its tenets. He was honest, courageous and self-controlled, and carried his uncompromising principles into public life. At the same time he exemplified the less attractive side of Stoicism; he was hard, unadaptable and lacking in humanity, and he provided a striking instance of the Stoic freedom from emotions in his matrimonial relations. He divorced his wife Marcia in order to give her to Hortensius, and later, after Hortensius's death, married her again; and it is clear from his admirer Lucan that his very coldness and lack of feeling were part of his philosophy, to be admired by its adherents. *Urbi pater est urbique maritus.** Pleasure, says Lucan, nowhere entered into his actions.⁴ A true Stoic like Cato was a man whom it was easier to admire than to love, and one who did not get much enjoyment out of life.

The fundamental principle of Stoicism was living in conformity with nature. Nature, however, is an ambiguous guide. The Sophists of the fifth century B.C. had set it up in opposition to man-made laws and conventions. Aristotle had denied this

* For Rome he became father, for Rome husband.

opposition when he claimed that man was by nature a 'political animal', and that the state was naturally prior to the individual. The Cynics rebelled against human society in all its aspects and pointed as a model to the natural life of animals. The Stoics had a different and a new interpretation of nature. They held that to be in conformity with nature was to live a life of virtue. Man's nature was a part of universal nature, which was guided and governed by the universal law of reason. Man's duty was to put himself in harmony with the universe, and since the universe was rational and good this meant that he must guide himself by reason and goodness.

The Epicureans also started from nature. Every living creature, they said, seeks after pleasure and avoids pain.[5] This, according to the critics, reduced man to the level of the beasts, and certainly Epicurean theory drew no clear distinction between mankind and other living things. This distinction the Stoics were above all anxious to maintain. They too started with the instinct shared with other animals, the natural desire for self-preservation; but man, they held, passed beyond this fundamental basic instinct as he grew up and developed his moral sense. His true kinship was not with the beasts but with the gods, for he was possessed of something the beasts had not, reason.

This reason was manifested in speech. For the Epicurean, human speech had gradually developed from the natural sounds by which animals no less than men make their feelings known. For the Stoic, it was a distinguishing mark of mankind, the expression of his rational powers. Reason was shown too in man's powers of logical thought and of forming general concepts, in his perception of moral values and his ability to conceive the idea of God. All these powers distinguished man from the beasts. Even his body marked the difference; his erect posture, with head raised on high, separated him from the beasts of the field and signified his kinship with the gods and the supremacy of reason within him.

Thus the Stoics held a high view of human nature. But if high it was also somewhat bleak. The ideal for mankind, at any rate as presented by the early Stoics, was narrow and limited. Man, to fulfil himself, must follow the highest part of himself, reason, that is, must live according to virtue. This was the only thing that mattered. Virtue was the only good and well-being depended on it alone. All other things which were generally accounted goods, health, pleasure, good looks, strength, wealth and reputation, even life itself, were of no account; they were things indifferent. The Stoic wise man must concentrate on the one thing necessary. And in doing so he would develop only one side of man's nature, the moral sense; the emotional side of man, his aesthetic feelings and his social instincts would be starved. The Stoic would not share the normal feelings of mankind. He would not sorrow at the loss of a friend or pity another's misfortunes; such feelings were both irrational (for losses and misfortunes were not real evils) and inconsistent with his constancy and self-control. He would not even be ἐπιεικής, kindly and amiable.[6]

The Stoic, however, had to live in this world, and did not entirely withdraw from it or deny it. The wise man was advised to marry and produce children. Zeno, it is true, in his *Politeia*, or Ideal State, permitted incest, and Chrysippus followed him, but later Stoicism rejected such radical tendencies, and even the earlier Stoics seem to have decided that whatever might be the case in an ideal state, in the world as it was the wise man should accept the institutions of marriage and the family and the responsibilities they involved. The wise man was also advised to play his part in public life. He would perform, they said, the functions of a citizen, and this in a Greek state implied some political activity.[7] The Stoics did not commit themselves to any precise political doctrine; what mattered to them was not the form but the spirit. But at any rate they did not, as did the Epicureans, warn their adherents off political activity, and their ideal for man implied a moral effort which, in a Roman at any rate, would naturally make itself felt in public life.

To those intellectual and literary accomplishments which were, in general, so highly prized in the ancient world the Stoics were perhaps rather more sympathetic than the Epicureans. Zeno had said that one could do without the liberal arts, but Chrysippus had corrected him, holding that these arts were useful and could lead to virtue, and Cicero in *De Finibus* attributes to the Stoics the view that the arts have a value in themselves because they involve the use of cognition and methodical reasoning.[8] On the other hand there was always a more radical side to Stoicism which at times asserted itself, and which tended to depreciate such activities as frivolous distractions.

Stoicism was indeed many-sided. The basic doctrines remained; the authority of Zeno and Chrysippus was unimpaired, but with different teachers the tone of the teaching could vary as much as that of Christianity has done. The Stoa could accommodate the harsh, fanatical preacher and the liberal, tolerant scholar. In the time of Cicero it was in the main the latter aspect that was to the fore, thanks to the influence of two remarkable men, both well known at Rome, Panaetius and Posidonius. Panaetius had nothing of the rigid doctrinaire attitude of earlier Stoicism. He was an admirer of Plato and cultivated the literary graces; he questioned some parts of Stoic orthodoxy, and by his emphasis on the ordinary, everyday duties of man gave a new turn to Stoic morality. He was on intimate terms with the leading Romans of his day, and it may well be supposed that his outlook was influenced by his association with men like Scipio Aemilianus; his moral teaching, as recorded by Cicero in *De Officiis*, seems typically Roman, a code of conduct for a governing class rather than a universal message for mankind in general.

The subject of Panaetius's treatise, which Cicero followed, was a kind of second best morality, suited to the ordinary man, as opposed to the counsels of perfection suited to the wise man. In it Stoic ideals were modified not a little by an insistence on the sense of fitness or propriety, τὸ πρέπον or *decorum* in Cicero's version, as something which should accompany and guide one in every sphere of virtuous action. In accordance with Stoic principles this is explained as conduct consistent with man's nature, that is, with the qualities in which man differs from the animals, the possession of reason and the moral sense. But in Panaetius we find a further extension of the idea of *decorum* which was not, it seems, a part of original Stoicism. Not only is there a universal decorum for all, but there is a particular one for particular persons. There are many differences of character, and one should make allowances for these and act as befits them, provided that one observes the general standards common to all mankind. 'What is most peculiar to each person is what most befits him.'[9] Not that Panaetius wished to justify eccentricity or extreme individualism. Apart from the general decorum common to all mankind, one's profession or position in life makes certain demands on one, as does one's age or status. Certain duties belong to the old, the young, magistrates, private citizens; others to certain places and times. In society one should observe the conventions, be cleanly and neat, not too careful, or too careless, of one's appearance. 'No one should make the mistake of supposing that if Socrates or Aristippus have done or said anything contrary to the manners and customs of society he may do the same.' The Cynics with their defiance of convention are firmly put in their place.[10] It is clear that in Panaetius's teaching there was a marked change of tone from that of the earlier Stoics, a new elasticity and readiness to compromise with the standards of ordinary life.

Posidonius, Panaetius's pupil and successor, was perhaps an even more remarkable man. He was versatile and learned, a historian and a traveller, a man of scientific interests who calculated the circumference of the earth and proved the connection between the tides and the phases of the moon, but one who combined the curiosity of the scientist with a strong religious feeling and a love of eloquent writing. He took all knowledge for his province, and drew together the theories of his day into an impressive synthesis. Unfortunately he remains a somewhat elusive figure, for his works can only be reconstructed from later authorities, and it is easier to suspect his influence than to prove it.

From Panaetius or Posidonius, or a combination of the two, comes that picture of the universe which Cicero gives in the second book of *De Natura Deorum* as the Stoic contribution to the debate on the nature of the gods. Here Stoicism appears in its most attractive guise. Balbus, the Stoic spokesman, sets out to prove the existence of divinity and to show its nature; he then proceeds to prove that divine providence governs the universe and that all is devised for man's good. The heavens declare the glory of god and the firmament showeth his handiwork. In the same spirit as the psalmist the Stoic surveys the wonders of the universe and finds in them clear evidence of the divine hand. As the works of man cannot exist without the hand and brain of the artificer, so the universe proclaims itself to be the work not of chance but of reason.[11] Balbus contemplates in admiration the beauties of nature, the earth with its infinite variety, clothed with flowers and fruits, with its springs and rivers, rocks, mountains and broad plains, its beasts and birds and mineral wealth. 'What of man, ordained to be the cultivator of the earth, allowing it neither to become the savage haunt of wild beasts of prey nor a barren waste of thicket and brambles, man by whose labour fields, islands and shores glitter with a diverse array of cities.'[12] The beauty of the sea, its islands and coasts and the creatures it bears, the alternation of day and night, the variety of the seasons, the majesty of the starry heavens all show the divine providence.

We turn to animal and vegetable life and find all marvellously adapted for the preservation of each species.[13] But the height of creation is man, for whom all is created.[14] Man's body, with its intricate mechanism and various parts so well adapted to their purpose, shows the divine hand; much more does his power of reason, his capacity for sense perception and his gift of speech. Then there are the hands, man's best servants, with which he produces paintings and sculpture and musical sounds, with which he tills the fields, builds houses, makes clothing and metal work and provides himself with food. Man's reason reaches even into the heavens; alone of living creatures he knows the risings and settings of the stars and the movements of the seasons and foretells eclipses of sun and moon.[15]

All that man makes use of is created for his benefit. The heavenly bodies, necessary for the stability of the universe, are also designed for men to observe. The fruits of the earth, which man alone is able to use to the full, are provided for him. Animals too are made for his use; sheep have no other purpose than to provide man with clothing, dogs are made to serve their human masters; oxen, mules and asses, even the wild beasts whom man hunts and tames, are created for him.[16]

There was of course much that could be said in criticism of this teleological explanation, and it was said, both by the Academics and by the Epicureans. Cicero regarded the Academics as the only opponents worth considering,[17] but posterity remembers rather the Epicurean criticisms, for Epicureanism had a great poet as an advocate. As one reads the eloquent periods which Cicero puts into the mouth of Balbus, one cannot forget Lucretius's four words *tanta stat praedita culpa,* so faulty is the universe. Much of the earth, he argues, is useless to man; what is of use he can only subdue to his service by hard work, and even then disasters overwhelm him and destroy the fruits of his labour. How then can the world be made for mankind by divine agency?[18]

Whether Stoics or Epicureans had the best of the argument, there is no doubt which of the two schools gave the more encouraging picture of life. Lucretius contemplates the naked helpless infant, like a shipwrecked sailor filling the place with wailing, as well it might, considering what ills it must experience in the passage through life.[19] The Stoic view, on the other hand, which made man the centre of the universe and the lord of creation, is optimistic and confident. There is a striking passage in Balbus's exposition in which he celebrates the achievements of man:

We place burdens and yokes on the backs of some animals, we use the marvellously sharp senses of elephants and the keen scent of dogs for our own purposes, we draw from the caverns of the earth the iron, so necessary for tilling the soil, we discover the deep hidden veins of copper, silver and gold, so fit for use and so comely for adornment; we cut up trees and use every kind of timber wild and cultivated, partly for fires to warm the body and for cooking, partly for building, so that by the protection of houses we may ward off cold and heat. Great are its uses too for building ships, by whose voyages all kinds of produce are supplied from every source: the most violent forces produced by nature, the sea and the winds, are tamed by man alone through his skill in navigation, and many are the products of the sea which we enjoy and use. The mastery of the

gifts of the earth is wholly in man's hands. We enjoy the
plains and the mountains; ours are the rivers and the lakes,
we sow corn and plant trees, we give fertility to the earth
by irrigation, we dam, straighten and divert the rivers, by
our hands we attempt to create in nature a new nature.[20]

How seldom we find this confident tone in ancient authors.
So often the conquest of nature is seen as arrogant presumption,
and seafaring and mining are condemned as prompted only by
greed. So often too admiration is reserved for man's purely
intellectual achievements as opposed to his technical skills, for
the head rather than the hand. The Stoics of the Middle
period, those who were most closely in touch with Republican
Rome, saw the hand as the instrument of the head, and the
techniques by which man controls nature as signs of the
operation of reason. Panaetius saw in the arts of civilized life
evidence of the powers of man, and used them to prove his
predominance in the universe and the mutual interdependence
of mankind.[21] Posidonius wrote of the invention of building,
tools and metals, of weaving, husbandry and bakery, all of
which he attributed to philosophy, that is, to human reason.[22]
The Stoic view that the earth and its products were made for
man implied the approval of the arts by which man made use
of these gifts.[23]

Thus as Stoicism developed in the period of the later Roman
Republic, it lost something of the narrowness of Zeno and
Chrysippus. It provided a confident and optimistic view of a
universe guided by divine providence with man in the centre,
master of creation, gifted with reason, developing all his faculties
for the organization of civilized society. It was a philosophy
that flattered man's self-esteem without outraging his reason,
a philosophy in which man's various instincts, social, artistic,
intellectual and religious, all found recognition. Yet for all its
apparent attractiveness, this form of Stoicism had an influence
which was comparatively short-lived; the fundamental character
of Stoicism was little affected, and the old message of Zeno and
Chrysippus outlived the new interpretations of their more
liberal and genial successors.

IV

POLITICAL THOUGHT

THE MAIN problems of philosophy remain more or less the same in all ages, and it was in no way surprising that the Romans, when they began to attend to such matters, should follow in the footsteps of the Greeks and think as they thought. But one side of Greek thought, that concerned with political theory, was so bound up with the circumstances of the Greek world that it could hardly be adopted by the Romans without some modification, or if it was so adopted was in danger of being irrelevant to Roman conditions. Greek political theory of the classical period, the theory of Plato and Aristotle, had been based on the city state; it was essentially anti-imperialistic, holding as it did to the ideal of the small self-sufficient pacific state, which provided in itself all the elements of the good life. Rome on the other hand, at the time when she came into contact with Greek theory, had long passed beyond the stage of the city state; she was also for better or worse the mistress of a great empire, and it was hardly to be expected that she would do anything but accept the situation.

Thus, respectful though the Romans might be to Plato and Aristotle, it was not likely that their political ideas would have more than a superficial influence. Nor was there a great deal that was relevant to Roman conditions to be learned from their successors. Post-Aristotelian political philosophy, so far as it followed the old lines, was timid and unenterprising, all too clearly affected by the failure of the city state. Democracy was dead, killed not so much by Plato's criticism as by its weakness in practice. To Polybius Athens was an example of a state that had ruined itself by its folly and inconstancy; his admiration was reserved for states which had shown greater powers of survival.[1] Reacting against the instability of the old city states,

thinkers were content to play for safety and regard stability as
the most important virtue of a state; and the old debate about
the relative merits of different types of government was settled
by a general agreement that the mixed constitution was the
best.

Roman political thinking begins with a Greek, Polybius,
who, observing the remarkable successes which had made Rome
in a short period mistress of almost the whole world, decided
that it was highly relevant to his task as a historian to study
the Roman system of government and Roman institutions.
Polybius had inherited many of the fundamental assumptions
of Greek political thought. He approached Rome with the
traditional classification of constitutions in mind (kingship,
aristocracy and democracy, with their corresponding corrupt
forms) and by convincing himself that the Roman constitution
included monarchical, aristocratic and democratic elements,
brought it into line with the orthodox belief in the virtues of
the mixed constitution.[2] He shared the common Greek view of
the moral and educational value of the laws of a state and,
following in the tradition of Plato, believed in an inevitable
cycle of constitutional change, and assumed that Rome would
follow this cycle and develop through democracy to mob rule.[3]
On the other hand, because he was a historian not a philosopher,
an observer rather than a teacher, he was better able than many
Greeks to understand Rome and to adapt Greek ideas to Roman
conditions. On the whole he had little of the doctrinaire about
him, and it may well be supposed that Scipio Aemilianus and
his friends, with whom he often discussed problems of politics,
would find themselves in agreement with him.[4] Certain points
they would have questioned. The Romans did not altogether
share Polybius's belief in the importance of constitutions,[5] and
laid more stress on men and manners. They would be unlikely
to accept his belief in the inevitability of cyclical change, and
unwilling to attach the same importance as he did to the
educational function of law. But they would have no difficulty
in sharing his view that the Roman state was the best in existence, and his sense of the gradual growth of Rome. Cato
remarked that Rome's superiority to other states lay in the fact

that whereas they had generally been the work of single legis-
lators, Rome was the product of the talents not of one man but
of many, and of a long period of history.[6] The point of view
seems essentially Roman, but it was shared by Polybius who,
contrasting Rome with Sparta, remarks that the Romans reached
the same results as Lycurgus not by a process of reasoning, but
as a result of many struggles and setbacks, by choosing the best
in the light of experience.[7]

Polybius's political ideas belong in the main to the tradition
of Plato and Aristotle. But the most influential schools were
now the new ones of the Hellenistic age, the Epicurean and
the Stoic. The Epicureans had nothing to offer in the sphere of
politics except the advice to avoid public life altogether. The
Stoics, however, had a more positive political doctrine. They
differed radically from the older Greek tradition. They did not
think in terms of the city state and were uninterested in constitutional forms.[8] Their characteristic ideas were the unity of
mankind and natural law. Men, they held, were united to one
another by the very fact of their common humanity, and being
thus bound together were naturally fitted for uniting in
societies.[9] And, while the Stoics commended the love and
service of one's fatherland, they preferred rather to dwell on
the greater community which consisted of the universe itself,
the common city of gods and men,[10] of which all were citizens,
ruled by the eternal and unchanging natural law which is based
on, indeed is identical with, reason.

The doctrines of Plato and Aristotle, the observations of
Polybius, the teaching of the Stoics, all find a place in Cicero's
De Republica. Though the combination of these ideas and their
adaptation to Rome is essentially Cicero's own, the spirit of the
dialogue is faithful to the setting in which it is placed, the circle
of Scipio Aemilianus. For it was in that circle that Roman men
of affairs and Greek intellectuals first met in friendly collabora-
tion and founded something in the nature of a tradition of
Roman political thinking, a tradition of which Cicero was glad
to be the inheritor.

Cicero's first task in De Republica was to justify political
activity against its detractors. The argument had its roots in

Greece, not so much in the conflict between the ideal of contemplation and that of political activity which was latent in
Plato and Aristotle, and which divided the Peripatetic school
in the post-Aristotelian period,[11] as in the individualism of the
Hellenistic schools which regarded political activity as conflicting with their ideal of personal happiness. In Cicero's day
it was the Epicureans who championed this view, and it was
probably they whom he had chiefly in mind when he wrote
the preface to *De Republica*. They had, one may suppose, no
little influence. The question whether one should or should not
take part in politics was by no means an academic one; Cicero's
friend Atticus had put the Epicurean doctrine into practice,
and may well have represented its attractions to Cicero at the
time he was writing *De Republica*, as we know he did some
years later.[12] The advocates of abstinence from political life
were ready with arguments and examples to show the hardships
and ingratitude which attend the politician, sounding, as
Cicero puts it, the signal for retreat to call back even those who
have already set out.[13] Cicero has no difficulty in answering
what he depicts as the arguments of selfish pleasure. The labours
of a politician's life, he maintains, are nothing to the man of
energy and industry, its dangers will not deter the brave man;
the service of the state is at once the fulfilment of a natural
instinct and a duty owed to the country which has given one
birth.[14]

Such is the theme of Cicero's preface. In the main part of the
first book the argument runs on familiar lines. The old debate
on the relative merits of monarchy, aristocracy and democracy
is renewed. The case for each is put in turn, and the conclusion
is the now familiar one that best of all is the mixed constitution. At the same time Cicero allows that any of the three
types is tolerable so long as it does not lose sight of the ultimate
object of the state. This recalls the Platonic and Aristotelian
distinction between the good and the bad forms of constitution.
Cicero's criterion for judging between good and bad forms is
by reference to his definition of the state. *Respublica* he had
defined as *res populi*, the affair of the people, the commonwealth
in the original sense of the word, and had explained that the

populus was a community joined together by common agreement on law and rights and by a desire to participate in mutual advantages, and that its origin was not self-interest but the natural instinct to combine in society.[15] The origin of the state must always be borne in mind and the bonds which unite society preserved.

We also find in the first book of *De Republica* some reference to the old Greek theory of constitutional cycles. In handling this Cicero wisely avoids any rigid scheme and allows for many variations[16] which bring the theory of cyclical development nearer to historical fact, while robbing it of much of its logical neatness. Cicero's belief was that the movements of the cycle were not inevitable, but could be foreseen and prevented by the wise statesman, who would avoid them by preserving the equilibrium of the state.[17] Here Roman experience modifies a Greek theory which was really of little relevance to Roman conditions.

At the end of the first book Scipio announces that there is no better state than the Roman; thus he will have fulfilled his task of describing the best state if he describes that of Rome. The hint was no doubt taken from Polybius, but by contrast with the professed political philosophers the method involved a new departure. Scipio is congratulated on having instituted a new manner of proceeding nowhere to be found in the Greek authorities, and his method is contrasted with that of Plato constructing his imaginary state remote from life and experience.[18] Here there is undoubtedly something characteristically Roman, for the Roman mind was more practical and empirical than the Greek, disposed to make do with the existing state of affairs and distrustful of *a priori* theorizing. It is characteristic too of Rome that Cicero's account of the Roman state is historical, an account of the development of its institutions from the earliest times, rather than analytical.

Plato and Aristotle had taken for granted that the state should provide all the elements of the good life, and had set no limits in theory to the functions of the lawgiver. In the ideal state the laws would perform an educational and moral function, would control and direct the lives of the citizens according to the principles of goodness and justice. Such an attitude belonged essentially to the city state, and was hardly relevant to a state of the size and character of Rome. However strong might be the Roman belief in the value of inherited tradition, Rome could not and did not attempt to impose a uniform outlook on her citizens. In the later Republic Rome was essentially a free, tolerant society. To take one important point, the Romans, as Polybius noted, had no state system of education;[19] it was not until the imperial period that official recognition was given to a system that had entered Rome originally not as a result of any deliberate policy on the part of the authorities but because the Romans were prepared to pay for what the Greek teachers offered.

With the works of Plato and Aristotle in mind Cicero could hardly avoid a discussion of the laws and institutions of the state. This subject he treated in the fourth book of *De Republica* and in *De Legibus*. His basic assumption was that Rome was the best of states and it was therefore inevitable that his main task should be not so much to legislate on the lines of the Greek theorists as to describe and justify Roman institutions. This he appears to have done in Book IV of *De Republica,* where among the fragments we find a number of criticisms of Greek practice and theory, while in *De Legibus,* although claiming to legislate for 'all sound and stable peoples',[20] he is quite clearly thinking of Roman conditions and basing himself on Roman practice.[21] His attitude was a mixture of a patriotic desire to stand up for Roman practice against Greek and a deference to the authority of Plato which leads him on occasion to emphasize, at the cost of some inconsistency, the moral and educational side of legislation. In *De Republica* he seems to have defended the Roman negligence in educational policy, contemptuously dismissing the theories of the Greeks, whereas in *De Legibus* he demands of the Senate a moral blamelessness which it did not have in reality, and expresses the hope that this end can be attained by education.[22] In *De Republica* he appears to prefer the rather vague authority of the Roman censor to the more detailed controls in force in Greek states or advocated by Greek authorities; in *De Legibus,* on the other hand, he is concerned to extend the powers of the censors to perform the functions of the Greek νομοφύλακες.²³ As regards the moral function of music, a matter on which one might well suppose him and other Romans to have been profoundly indifferent, he is prepared with only slight reservations to follow Plato.²⁴

In the last two books of the *Republic,* now, apart from the *Somnium Scipionis,* in a sadly fragmentary state, Cicero discussed the figure to whom he applies such terms as *rector, moderator* or *gubernator reipublicae.* What exactly Cicero had in mind in this part of his work is far from clear. Apart from the question of the relevance of his ideas to the immediate political situation, it is hard to say whether he was seriously proposing a modification of the Roman constitution which would strengthen the monarchical element, or whether he was rather depicting the ideal statesman without any special reference to constitutional arrangements. On the one side it can be said that in the first book Cicero puts the arguments for monarchy into the mouth of his chief character Scipio, and makes him express the view that if he must choose between the three types of constitution his preference is for monarchy; and this in connection with his equation of the *rector* with the ideal king as opposed to the tyrant suggests that he is arguing for an extension of the monarchical element in the constitution.²⁵ On the other hand, Cicero's own description of *De Republica* as being about the best form of state and the best citizen suggests that his purpose was simply to describe the qualities of the good statesman, as does the *Somnium Scipionis,* from which it appears that all who served their country might claim the title of *rectores reipublicae.*²⁶ Moreover, in Cicero's other writings we find him satisfied with the Roman constitution and suspicious of personal rule.

It may well be that even if we had *De Republica* in full we should still find some inconsistency and lack of clarity, due to Cicero's desire to do justice to the views of the various Greek philosophers who had preceded him. Greek political philosophy was by no means unsympathetic to monarchy. Plato's ideal was the philosopher king: Aristotle was prepared to allow that a man pre-eminent in virtue and ability should be regarded as above the law; while in the Hellenistic age, when monarchy was the normal form of government in the Greek-speaking world, philosophers were ready to expatiate on the virtues of the good king. The Roman tradition was firmly anti-monarchical, and if in *De Republica* Cicero flirted with monarchical ideas, he did so, it would seem, in deference to Greek theory rather than as a result of convictions drawn from his own experience of Roman conditions.

It remains to say something of Cicero's relation to Stoic ideas. It was in the third book of *De Republica,* where he discussed the nature of justice, that, so far as we can tell, he drew most on the Stoics. The issue had been raised in a provocative way by Carneades when he came on the embassy of 155 B.C. and gave his famous lectures, discoursing first in defence of justice, and then on the following day speaking on the opposite side. Cicero followed Carneades, though significantly the order of the argument is reversed, and the advocate of justice allowed to have the last word, while to avoid any suggestion that a respected Roman should deny the principles of morality, Philus, who plays the part of *advocatus diaboli*, is made to disclaim any belief in his own arguments.

Philus, following Carneades, argued that men's concepts of right differed in different parts of the world and in different ages. Law was based not on nature but on utility. There was no such thing as justice, or, if there was, it was sheer folly, since the man who considered others' interests did harm to his own. In reply Laelius, here Cicero's spokesman, asserts the Stoic idea of law in a lofty and impressive passage:

> There is in fact a true law, namely right reason, which is in accordance with nature, applies to all men, and is unchangeable and eternal. By its commands this law summons men to the performance of their duties; by its prohibitions it restrains them from doing wrong. Its commands and prohibitions always influence good men, but are without effect on the bad. To invalidate this law by human legislation is never morally right, nor is it permissible ever to restrict its operation, and to annul it wholly is impossible.

Neither senate nor people can absolve us from our obligation to obey this law, and it requires no Sextus Aelius to expound and interpret it. It will not lay down one rule at Rome and another at Athens, nor will it be one rule today and another tomorrow. But there will be one law, eternal and unchangeable, binding at all times on all peoples; and there will be as it were one common master and ruler of men, namely God, who is author of this law, its interpreter and its sponsor. The man who will not obey it abandons his better self and denies the true nature of man, thus suffering the worst of penalties, though he has escaped all the other consequences which men call punishments.[27]

Similar ideas are found in the first book of *De Legibus,* where Cicero, laying the philosophical foundations of the study of law, begins with the Stoic theme that man as the possessor of reason is allied not to the beasts but to the gods, and proceeds to argue that man is born for justice and that right is a matter not of opinion but of nature.[28] 'This will become plain if you get a clear conception of man's fellowship and union with his fellow men. No single thing is so like another, so exactly its counterpart, as all of us are to one another. . . . However we define man, the same definition applies to all; this is sufficient proof that there is no difference in kind between man and man. . . . Reason is common to all. . . . There is no human being of any race who cannot if he finds a guide attain to virtue.'[29] Thus man is made for a mutual relationship of justice; bad habits may corrupt the natural sense of right and extinguish the sparks implanted by nature, but if men followed their true nature all would follow justice.[30]

What, it might be asked, was the relation between these lofty ideas and the realities of Roman political life? Was Rome, the best of all states according to Cicero, guided by justice and reason? Carneades did not think so. For him imperialism inevitably involved injustice; it was by wrong doing and by seizing what belonged to others that Rome had gained possession of the world; if the Romans wished to be just, they would have to give up what they had taken from others, which would mean a return to a primitive life of poverty and misery.[31] In answer to these arguments, which he repeated in *De Republica,* Cicero apparently claimed that subjection was advantageous to the subject peoples and that the Romans had gained their Empire by defending their allies.[32] This part of the dialogue is in a very fragmentary state, but we can perhaps get some idea of Cicero's point of view from a later work, *De Officiis,* derived in the main from Panaetius. Panaetius, and Cicero after him, handled morality under the two heads of the good and the expedient. Carneades, in his argument 'against justice', had maintained that the two were incompatible; to seek one's own advantage, whether for individuals or for states, involved the disadvantage of others and was therefore unjust. Such an attitude was naturally unsympathetic to the Romans. Their conduct of affairs in the course of history had undoubtedly proved advantageous to themselves, but at the same time they were unwilling to think of themselves as anything but a just and fair-dealing people. So if it could be shown that there was no real conflict between the good and the expedient, they would naturally welcome the conclusion.

This was the view of Panaetius and the other Stoic authorities whom Cicero followed in *De Officiis.* Human society, so runs the argument, is based on nature; to harm others for one's own advantage is contrary to nature and therefore subversive of society. Nature ordains that one man should care for another simply because he is a man; what is in the interests of one is in the interests of all.[33] Therefore whatever is good is also expedient, and nothing can be expedient which is not good. In applying these principles to public conduct Cicero shows himself understandably influenced by his position as a member of the Roman governing class and by his patriotic desire to justify Rome's record. Justice, as explained in *De Officiis,* tends to become little more than the principles on which existing society is organized, particularly in respect to property. Indeed Cicero goes so far as to claim that the protection of property was the chief purpose of the establishment of states, in which perhaps he went further than his Stoic authorities warranted.[34] One notes also that while he condemns those who maintain that one should consider the interests of one's fellow citizens but not those of foreigners, elsewhere he mentions as one of the duties of a statesman that he should not impose a property tax on the people, a requirement which presupposes the conditions of Rome, drawing tribute from a subject empire.[35] He does, however, venture to make some criticism of Roman conduct in the light of his ideals. He expresses regret for the destruction of Corinth, and paints a gloomy picture of recent Roman history, comforting himself with looking back to an idealized past. Rome, he says, had once been just and merciful, but had declined from the high standards of the past. Once she had been protectress rather than mistress of the world; now 'we would rather be feared than loved'.[36]

Though its doctrine of natural law and the unity of mankind offered an ideal for society, Stoicism gave no guidance as to the means by which the ideal might be realized. Holding as they did that the bad were impervious to the influence of reason and that the rewards and punishments of this world were of no account, the Stoics were unlikely to put much trust in schemes for the reformation of society. The emphasis was all on the individual, and if the good man realized his highest nature and guided his life by the law of reason, this was as much as he could do.

Here the influence of Stoicism reinforced that of the Roman tradition. The Roman state, Ennius had said, rested on her ancient ways of life and her men, and Cicero endorses the saying as an utterance of oracular brevity and truth.[37] His final message is concerned with men rather than measures, when at the end of *De Republica* he makes an appeal for the disinterested service of the state in the *Somnium Scipionis*. The dream is one experienced by Scipio Aemilianus while in Africa. In it he finds himself with his grandfather by adoption, the elder Scipio Africanus, high up among the stars, and is told by him that there is a place in heaven reserved for those who have served their country, where they live for ever in bliss; nothing on earth pleases the ruler of the universe more than communities of men living in a commonwealth; those who guide and preserve such communities return to the heaven from which they originally came. The two are joined by Scipio's father in the flesh, Aemilius Paulus, who discourses on the nature of the universe and the music of the spheres, on the vanity of human glory and the immortality of the soul. Paulus's message reinforces that of Africanus; Scipio is urged to apply the immortal part of himself to the highest activity, that of ensuring the safety of the fatherland. The soul that has been so engaged will fly to its own home, the abode of the blessed among the stars.

The *Somnium Scipionis* is an interesting mingling of Greek and Roman elements. The philosophical ideas are Greek, partly Platonic, partly Stoic, but there are two features which are essentially Roman. Firstly there is the feeling for family tradition which finds expression in the meeting of Scipio with his father. Secondly there is the exaltation of political activity. The idea that there is a special place in heaven reserved for the good statesman is alien to Greek philosophy and is Cicero's own.

V

CICERO AND PHILOSOPHY

FOR MOST of his life philosophy was not in the forefront of Cicero's interests. He believed in a union of rhetoric with philosophy and of statesmanship with philosophy, and liked to think of himself as a philosophic orator and philosophic statesman, but oratory and statesmanship came first. It was only at the end of his life that philosophy was promoted to the first place in his interests, in the year 45 B.C., when he was sixty-one years old. Caesar was now dictator, and there was no room for Cicero in public life. Family troubles added to his unhappiness. He quarrelled with his brother, divorced his wife and lost his daughter. He turned to philosophy for comfort and, what was very characteristic of Cicero, turned to writing.[1]

Cicero has himself informed us in the preface to his philosophical works what were his reasons for writing. Firstly there was the desire to provide Rome with a philosophical literature. Hitherto there had been nothing worthy of Rome's achievements in other branches of literature; the Epicurean treatises of Amafinius and others were poorly written, and Cicero wanted to produce something better.[2] Secondly, he wished to educate his fellow countrymen. 'There is', he wrote, 'no greater or better service I can render the state than that of teaching and instructing the young.'[3] Finally, Cicero found in philosophical writing a kind of substitute for political activity. Being deprived of his former occupation he could occupy himself and relieve his mind by this means, and philosophical disputation filled the place of political debate.[4]

These declared reasons for writing do not give the impression that Cicero had any very definite message of his own, and such was indeed the case. He said of one at any rate of his books that his aim was to help people to understand what had been

54

said for and against each philosophy. Some of his readers complained that they could not discover what his own views were. He answered that they were showing unnecessary curiosity and rebuked them for not using their own judgment; he did not want his authority to stand in the way of preventing an impartial decision. He was no Pythagoras pronouncing his oracles to a believing band of disciples.[5]

None the less Cicero had a point of view, that of the Academic school, which stood for free inquiry, and the discovery of the truth, or at any rate of the most probable opinion, by criticism of the various current theories. In his youth Cicero had, it appears, been attracted to the Epicurean school; but it was not long before he turned with enthusiasm to the doctrines of the Academy as expounded by Philo.[6] Apart from any intellectual conviction he was naturally drawn to a school with a distinguished ancestry going back to Plato, for whom Cicero had the highest respect, and one which had maintained contact with the world of politics and literature,[7] while by temperament and by his forensic training he was disposed to see and to argue both sides of a case.

'It is our way', he writes, explaining the Academic point of view, 'to oppose all schools, and so we cannot object if others differ from us; though we have an easy case to argue, we who wish to discover the truth without contention and pursue it with all diligence and devotion. . . . Our arguments have as their sole purpose to discover and draw out something which may be either true or as near the truth as possible, by putting the case for either side. The only difference between us and the dogmatists is that they have no doubt of the truth of their case, whereas we consider many doctrines probable and are prepared to act on them, but hardly to affirm them as certain. We are more free and untrammelled in that our power of judgment is unimpaired.'[8] Cicero often returns to the theme of freedom of thought. 'Let each man defend what he believes; judgment is free.' ' "Quot homines tot sententiae"; we may be wrong.' 'There is no reason to object to the clash of argument; what is unworthy of philosophy is abuse, insult, anger and obstinate wrangling and fighting in argument.'[9] Cicero himself claims to be ready to refute without obstinacy and be refuted without anger. He does not even object to being convicted of inconsistency: 'We live for the day; whatever makes a strong impression of probability on us, that we assert, and thus we alone are free.'[10]

Cicero's attitude was already somewhat out of date when he wrote. Many of his contemporaries thought his philosophy to be one which, so far from shedding light on the problems of life, involved them in thick darkness, and expressed surprise at his championship of a point of view which had been abandoned.[11] Even in the Academy the attitude of detached scepticism was now a thing of the past. Under Antiochus, who had succeeded Cicero's master Philo as head of the school, it had drawn close to Stoicism; the Stoics, according to Antiochus, were really saying the same thing as Plato and Aristotle though in different words. Cicero himself, though he supported the older generation, the 'New' Academy of Carneades and his followers, against Antiochus in the matter of the problem of knowledge, showed not a little sympathy with the new trends, and at times came close to the Stoics, or actually followed them, as in *De Officiis*.

On the whole in his philosophical works he followed the method of debate. In *De Finibus* the doctrines of the Epicureans and the Stoics are expounded in turn, followed in each case by criticism, and finally there is a statement of the views of Antiochus, without any formal or extended criticism. In *De Natura Deorum* we again have an exposition of the Stoic and Epicurean points of view, with criticisms from the Academy, which is here seen as purely negative and destructive. The last word is left with the critic of Stoicism, though Cicero informs us in a brief sentence that he himself inclines to the Stoic view.[12] *De Divinatione* is on the same lines as *De Natura Deorum*, except that here there is no statement of the Epicurean doctrine, which indeed was unnecessary as the Epicureans denied divination altogether; Cicero first gives a defence of divination on Stoic lines, then an attack on it, derived from an Academic source. Cicero's other important philosophic works, the *Tusculan Disputations* and *De Officiis*, are of a somewhat different character. In the *Tusculans,* though the dialogue form is kept, there is little of the clash of doctrines; a theme is announced only to be demolished, and argument tends to give way to exhortation. In *De Officiis* the dialogue form is abandoned altogether and Cicero appears as the teacher rather than the critical expositor.

In this last work Cicero followed a Stoic authority. He explains that this does not involve any inconsistency with his sceptical position. He was not, he says, one of those whose minds wander vaguely without any fixed aim; though he was prepared only to call things probable rather than certain, there was nothing to prevent him from adhering to the more probable view.[13] He evidently found it hard to resist the logic of the Stoic case. The main controversy of the day (leaving aside the Epicureans) was between the Stoics, who held that virtue was the sole good and therefore sufficient for the blessed life, and those who allowed the existence of other goods. Among the latter was Antiochus, who, claiming to go back to the ancients, the philosophers before Zeno, held that man's *summum bonum* was a life containing all the goods of body as well as of mind, though the latter were the most important; virtue by itself was enough to make one blessed, but not supremely blessed. Antiochus's view seemed to Cicero unsatisfactory; if there were goods other than virtue, he did not see how one could call the wise man blessed, because on that view bodily pain and poverty would be ills, and, if they were ills, the wise man could not but be in a state of unhappiness if ill or poor.[14] Thus Cicero is on the side of the Stoics on this point, though in the *Tusculans* he does not insist on the argument, but maintains that the thesis that virtue is sufficient for happiness is compatible with all philosophies.[15]

Cicero's attitude to philosophy is hard to define, for it varied with the mood of the moment. Under the influence of private grief he persuaded himself for a time that philosophy was the highest activity of man. In the *Hortensius,* his exhortation to the life of philosophy, now unfortunately lost, he praised the pursuit of truth as the most worthy aim of mankind and the source of true happiness. 'If after this life is ended we were to live for ever in the Isles of the Blest of which legend tells, what need would there be for eloquence, when there would be no law courts? Or even for the moral virtues? . . . One thing would give us happiness, the discovery and knowledge of nature, which alone makes the life of the gods praiseworthy.'[16] This is a point of view which, though familiar enough in Greek philosophy, would hardly be acceptable to the Romans. It was in direct conflict with the Roman tradition of service to the state, and with Cicero's own attitude in *De Republica*. And Cicero himself, though no doubt he felt convinced at the time of writing, was not really converted. The unworldly spirit in which he first approached philosophy passed away. He recovered from his grief, and as he recovered his attitude changed. In the *Academica* he wrote: 'Now that I have been smitten by a grievously heavy blow of fortune, and am also released from my share in the conduct of government, I seek in philosophy a cure for grief and deem it too the worthiest way of employing my leisure.'[17] In *De Divinatione*, written a year later, there is less emphasis on the blows of fortune and the need for a cure for grief, and more on the value of his work as a service to the state.[18] Philosophy was the haven in which he took refuge from the storms of life,[19] but he was ready to put out to sea again when the storms had abated. In sending *De Officiis* to his son he seems to regard his philosophical work with a certain indifference and to be mainly anxious to commend his literary abilities.[20] It should not be forgotten that *De Officiis* was finished after the assassination of Caesar, and the prospect of a return to political life was now opening before Cicero. Philosophy yielded to politics; the philosopher's cloak gave way to the toga, the preaching of the *Tusculans* to the invective of the *Philippics*.

Cicero's attitude also varied with the subject he was treating. When dealing with disputed questions of theory he appears as the Academic seeker after truth. But in his day philosophy was something more than an intellectual discipline; it was a guide to living. It claimed to heal the soul and remove vain worries, to free man from desires and drive away fears. Those who obeyed its laws would be armed for ever against fortune, would possess in themselves all the means of a good and happy life, and would be in a perpetual state of happiness.[21] The wise man would despise pain, be free from fear and irrational emotions, would rise superior to all mental pain, be indifferent to poverty and exile, even happy under torture; independent of circumstances, he would be armed to meet all the blows of fortune. Such was the ideal of the Stoics, shared to some extent by the philosophers of other schools. And when Cicero read their exhortations and reproduced them, as he did in the *Tusculans,* he fell under the spell of this heroic attitude. He had indeed some doubts. 'When I consider these disasters in which fortune has so severely tested me, I begin at times to doubt this view (that virtue is sufficient for the blessed life) and to fear the weakness and frailty of human kind. I fear that nature, when she gave us weak bodies and joined to them incurable diseases and intolerable pains, may have given us minds too in conformity with the pains of the body as well as involved in their own afflictions and annoyances. But here I blame myself for judging of the strength of virtue by the weakness of others, and perhaps of myself too, not by virtue itself.' His doubts had been removed by the example of Cato. The fault, he decided, lay not in nature but in himself. To strengthen himself and correct his faults and errors he takes refuge in philosophy. 'O philosophy, guide of life, you who discover the way to virtue and banish vices, what should we have been, and not only we but the very life of man, without you? . . . I fly to you, seek help from you and to you commit myself, as I did to a large extent before now but now do wholly and entirely. For one day led well and in accordance with your precepts is to be preferred before an immortality of vice.'[22]

The exalted tone of this passage is noticeably absent from *De Officiis.* Here, as we have seen, Cicero took as his main guide Panaetius, a man who as a friend and adviser of a cultured and enlightened aristocracy at a time when the Roman Republic seemed still stable and flourishing, saw the task of philosophy as the provision of a workable moral code for everyday life rather than the strengthening of the soul to meet adversity. Cicero with his remarkable capacity for changing from one mood to another caught the tone of the friend of

Scipio, and his last utterance on human conduct shows a Stoicism less heroic and less unworldly, but more humane, than that of the *Tusculans,* a philosophy not for exceptional men and abnormal crises, but for ordinary men living in ordinary times.

If there are changes of mood between one of Cicero's philosophical works and another, there are also differences of outlook between his philosophical and his non-philosophical writings. We have observed in an earlier chapter the contrasts between the formal education of the Roman of Cicero's day, Greek in content and outlook, appealing to the reason rather than the emotions, and the national traditions which still had some force in moulding the Roman character. If the purpose of education is to free one from the limitations of nationality and to make one intellectually a citizen of the world, there was much to be said for this system. But it had its disadvantages. It meant that the Roman tended to live in two worlds, the Greek world of rational, intellectual speculation and the Roman world of sentiment and tradition, and that the two were never completely harmonized. One can see this particularly in the matter of religion. In *De Natura Deorum* the characters in the dialogue discuss the matter on purely Greek lines; they treat the nature of the gods as a purely intellectual problem and make little reference to the established Roman religion. But when he left his study and entered the forum the Roman would forget his Greek reading and surrender to the Roman tradition. We have already seen how Cicero in his speeches took the state religion for granted. Who is to say which is the real Cicero, the student in his study discussing dispassionately and sceptically the nature of deity or the orator appealing to Jupiter of the Capitol and the other gods who have guided the state from time immemorial?

Cicero himself has given us an indication of the Roman attitude in religious matters in the words he puts in the mouth of Cotta in *De Natura Deorum*: 'I will always defend, and always have defended, the traditional Roman religious opinions, rites and ceremonies, and nothing that anyone, learned or unlearned, says will move me from the views I have inherited from our forefathers about the worship of the immortal gods.

On any question of religion I follow men who held the office of pontifex maximus, like Coruncanius, Scipio and Scaevola, not Zeno, Cleanthes or Chrysippus. . . . I have never held that any branch of traditional Roman religion should be despised, and am persuaded that Romulus by establishing the auspices and Numa by instituting our sacred rites laid the foundations of our state, which could never have been so great as it is if the favour of the immortal gods had not been ensured.'[23] It is customary to emphasize the weakness of Roman religion in the time of Cicero, and to suppose that the state rites were kept up mainly for political reasons by men who were unbelievers or at least sceptics in religion. But it may be that we overestimate the importance of the enlightened scepticism which we find displayed in Cicero's treatises, and that there were many, like Cotta, with whom the Roman tradition was more powerful than rational argument. Roman religion was in a sense in a strong position against intellectual criticism, for having no creeds it had no intellectual position to defend; and it had a powerful ally in patriotic sentiment. It should be remembered too that even for those interested in intellectual enquiry philosophy was an importation from outside, learned and read for the most part in Greek, and so kept in a separate compartment of the mind.

The conflict between two different ways of thought can be illustrated further from Cicero's attitude to divination. In his dialogue on the subject he is himself the spokesman of scepticism, and undoubtedly has the best of the argument. He appears to be a complete sceptic to those who read only *De Divinatione*; but he was himself an augur, and when he wrote as a statesman, in *De Legibus*, he showed himself much more sympathetic to divination. When he has explained the importance of the augur's functions, Atticus is made to draw attention to the difference of opinion on the part of the authorities, some of whom supported augury purely on political grounds, others on the ground that it was a means of divination. Cicero gives his opinion, somewhat hesitatingly, in favour of the latter view, and asserts his belief in divination. 'If the gods exist, and guide the universe and care for mankind and can give us indications of future events, I see no reason for denying divination.'[24]

Augury, along with the other religious institutions of Rome,
is maintained in the legislation of the *Laws*.

Here we see Cicero drawn in two different directions by the
two different traditions which he inherited, the Roman and the
Greek. Where the former had nothing to say he could follow
the philosophers with less hesitation. So it was in the matter of
the survival of the soul after death.[25] His discussion of the
matter in the first book of the *Tusculans* reveals some un-
certainty in the face of the diverse theories of the philosophers,
but one thing Cicero is prepared to assert, that the soul is divine,
which is another way of saying that it is immortal.[26] In general
Plato is Cicero's guide rather than the later philosophers. The
belief in survival that he expresses was alien to the ways of
thought of his day. The contemporary philosophies were
centred in this world. The Epicureans denied life after death
entirely, and the Stoics, while they might hold that the divine
substance which constituted the human soul was united at
death with the world soul, laid little stress on survival and
rejected the traditional ideas of rewards and punishments,
holding the austere view that virtue was its own reward and
vice its own punishment. Panaetius, the most eminent Stoic
of his day, had denied the survival of the soul altogether.[27]
Posidonius, it is true, did not follow his master in this respect,
and may well have played his part in preparing the way for
Cicero, but it seems probable that it was the direct influence
of Plato which was mainly responsible for Cicero's outlook.

The Platonic arguments evidently made a strong impression
on him, and on this subject at any rate he speaks with some
degree of personal conviction. In the *Somnium Scipionis* Scipio
is told: 'Be assured then that you are not mortal. Only your
body is mortal; you are not what your appearance shows you
to be; each man is his mind, not the outer form which can be
pointed to with the finger. Know then that you are a god, if
god is what is active, what feels, remembers, foresees, and
guides and governs and moves the body over which it presides,
as the great god does over the universe.'[28] Again, in the
Consolatio Cicero wrote that whatever it is that has feeling,
knowledge, life, activity, must be of heavenly origin and divine,

and therefore immortal, and the same ideas appear in *De Senectute,* where Cato is made to speak with an assurance which evidently belongs rather to Cicero.[29] And when Cato looks forward to meeting his son who had died before him and whose soul had passed to those regions where Cato himself must soon come, it is easy to recognize the voice and the feelings of Cicero himself as he remembers his daughter Tullia.[30]

As regards the conduct of life there was no great conflict between Roman traditions and Greek ideals for those who accepted Stoicism or, like Cicero, were sympathetic to it. Cato was at once a thorough Stoic and a Roman statesman. He carried his philosophy into the senate house in a very literal sense—he would read Stoic books while waiting for business to begin[31]—and he used not a little of it in his public speeches. He spoke as a Stoic on such themes as greatness of soul, self-control, death and the praise of virtue; only such esoteric doctrines as the paradoxes he would leave alone.[32] Cicero too regarded philosophy as a source to supply his oratory with material on the moral virtues,[33] and though we have already suggested that the debt to philosophy was not very great, the virtues he praises in public were certainly not inconsistent with those commended by the philosophers. When discoursing on the conduct of life in his philosophical treatises he is at particular pains to introduce illustrations from Roman history, showing thereby that the message of philosophy was not something alien to or inconsistent with ancestral traditions. The Roman heroes are brought in too to point the argument against the Epicureans, whose rejection of virtue for pleasure is thus shown to be contrary to Roman traditions.

Yet there was at least one point on which Cicero must have felt some conflict between his philosophy and his Roman upbringing. The longing for glory, the desire to leave a name to posterity, was a marked feature of the Roman temperament and was present to an abnormal degree in Cicero himself. To the philosopher, however, worldly glory was something to be despised. It is hard to reconcile Cicero's frank admission of his desire for glory in his speech for Archias with the words of Africanus in the *Somnium Scipionis* on the vanity of human fame.[34] *Philosophiae quidem praecepta noscenda, vivendum autem civiliter.*[*][35] The remark, quoted from a letter of Cicero to his son, suggests that there were times when he felt that tradition provided a better guide to life than philosophy.

Cicero's philosophical works leave us with mixed feelings. He himself has said the worst that can be said of them: 'They are copies, done with little labour; I only add the words, of which I have an abundance.'[36] Certainly there is much hasty work in them; there are changes of mood which leave us bewildered, and an indifference to consistency which verges on irresponsibility. None the less the works are impressive, if only as evidence of the high culture of the age. At no time were the Romans better read in philosophy or more keenly interested in it. It may be that under the Empire philosophy was a more powerful influence in moulding men's lives, but in the late Republic it was combined with a general culture and an active political life in a way that is hardly found later. Cicero himself is the great example of this all-round culture, but we should not forget that many other leading statesmen of the period had philosophical interests. Crassus had devoted some attention to philosophy. Pompey showed his respect for philosophers by gifts of money and by listening to their discourses.[37] Cato was well known as a Stoic; Brutus was attached to the Academy, and Cassius was an Epicurean. There were indeed some who disapproved of philosophy, or approved it only in moderation; there were also those who disapproved of Cicero's philosophic writings, either on the grounds that philosophy should be read in Greek or because to write on such a subject did not befit a man of Cicero's rank. But Cicero, who answered such objections in the preface to *De Finibus*, seems to have overcome such lingering prejudices, and if his writings provoked some criticism they also provoked interest and encouraged many to study.[38]

Among the Roman followers of philosophy in the last years of the Republic there is one name that deserves special mention, that of Cato, for Cato not only lived but died in accordance with the precepts of philosophy. If anyone is tempted to think of philosophy in the Ciceronian age as nothing more than the

---

* One should know what philosophy teaches, but live like a gentleman.

amusement of the dilettante in his leisure hours, he should read the account of Cato's last hours in Plutarch's life. He had with him two philosophers, one a Stoic and one a Peripatetic. They were among the company at supper and the talk ran on philosophic questions. Over the wine 'one philosophical tenet after another made the rounds, until there came up the enquiry into what were called the "paradoxes" of the Stoics, namely that the good man alone is free and that the bad are all slaves'. The Peripatetic raised objections to the paradoxes, 'whereupon Cato broke in with vehemence and in loud and harsh tones maintained his argument at the greatest length and with astonishing earnestness, so that everyone perceived that he had made up his mind to put an end to his life and free himself from his present troubles.'[39]

The supper came to an end; Cato walked with his friends for a little, gave the officers their instructions, then retired to his room and took up Plato's *Phaedo*. He asked for his sword to be brought; the servant did not bring it, and Cato went on with the *Phaedo* until it was finished. Then his son and others came in, hoping to dissuade him from his purpose, but eventually he was left alone with the two philosophers. He told them that he had as yet come to no decision, but when he did it would be with the aid of philosophy. The two departed and left him alone. Now his sword was brought in. He examined it, saw that its edge was sharp and said, 'Now I am my own master'. Then he read the *Phaedo* again and fell asleep. It was already morning when he drew his sword and stabbed himself. At once the people of Utica assembled and 'with one voice they called Cato their saviour and benefactor, the only man who was free, the only one unvanquished'.[40]

The commendations of the people of Utica were echoed by Stoics and others in following years. Cato's death proved that Stoic virtue was not an impossible ideal and that the wise man could be found on this earth. In the early Empire it was he rather than Cicero who was remembered, for while Cicero had written about philosophy Cato had lived and died as a philosopher should. Example counted for more than precept; the saint was more influential than the scholar.

PHILOSOPHY IN THE
AUGUSTAN AGE

THE INTEREST aroused by Cicero's philosophical works was probably short-lived. Cicero had hoped to interest and educate the younger generation, but in fact most of his readers, so it appears, were drawn from his contemporaries. Among the elderly he had more readers than he expected; of the young he can only express the hope that a few will listen to him, and that those few will have a wide influence.[1] Even this modest hope seems hardly to have been fulfilled in the years that followed. Some centuries later one of Cicero's works proved a decisive influence on St Augustine, and later still, after the revival of learning, Cicero performed just the sort of educative function that he hoped to have in his own day. But in the period immediately following his death, the period of the triumvirs and the principate of Augustus, there is little evidence that his philosophical works had any great influence. They sum up the culture of the Republican age that was ending; they do not look forward to the new age that was opening.

'What', asked the rhetorician Haterius, 'has Cicero in common with an alien generation?'[2] The words apply in the intellectual as well as in the political sphere. The Augustan age was not frivolous—in some ways it was more serious than the age of Cicero; but it asked of philosophy something different from what Cicero had to offer. Cicero offered debate and discussion and the impartial weighing of opposing views. The Augustans were tired of argument. *Et nunc cedo equidem pugnasque exosa relinquo.**[3] Philosophic strife was as out of keeping with the spirit of the age as political strife.

The old sharp distinctions between the various schools were

---

* Well, now I yield and, loathing, quit the strife. (RHOADES)

now blurred. The process had begun in the time of Cicero; in the age that followed it was carried further. The characteristic outlook of the Augustan age is a synthesis of various philosophical points of view. Vitruvius, when he describes the rise of man from a primitive beast-like existence, the development of language and the discovery of fire, seems to be following in general outline the Epicurean theory as set out by Lucretius.[4] When, however, he speaks of men being gifted by nature with an upright posture enabling them to behold the glories of the heavens, and refers to the 'divine mind' which constituted the universe, we get the impression rather of a Stoic.[5] Vitruvius could take his philosophy from the two rival schools without any feeling of inconsistency. So too Propertius can look forward to amending his life in the groves of Plato or the garden of Epicurus without apparently any consciousness that there was a radical difference between the teaching of the two masters.[6]

In this atmosphere of relative indifference to philosophical distinctions the strongest school, that of the Stoics, tended to prevail. The Epicureans, so active and so powerful in the last years of the Republic, lost ground rapidly and decisively, and by the time that Augustus was established as ruler of Rome they had ceased to be of any importance as an intellectual influence. It is the Stoics to whom men listen and whose books they read; it was Stoicism that Damasippus learned from Stertinius and Davus from Crispinus's doorkeeper; Stoic books lay among the pillows of the lady attacked by Horace in *Epode* VIII, and it was the works of the Stoic Panaetius that his friend Iccius collected.[7] The two great figures of Augustan literature, Virgil and Horace, were both influenced by Epicureanism in their early years, and though neither of them definitely adhered to Stoicism, they both moved away from the creed of their youth.

Throughout his life Horace retained an interest in philosophy, or at any rate in moral theory, and as he had a way of committing his thoughts to writing it is possible to follow their development from the time of the triumvirate onwards. The impression we get from the *Satires* is that Epicureanism is now on the defensive. It had been otherwise in the time of Cicero, when Amafinius and his followers were read all over Italy. Now it is the Stoics who are active in propaganda, men like Fabius, Crispinus and Stertinius, preachers with a striking paradoxical message, ridiculous perhaps, but insistent and not to be ignored. Horace himself in his earlier satires appears as an Epicurean. In the *Journey to Brundisium* he proclaims his adherence to the school in words that echo Lucretius, *namque deos didici securum agere aevum*;* and in the third satire of the first book he uses the Epicurean theory of the origin of society to argue against the Stoic view that all virtues, and all vices, are equal.[8] But by the time he wrote the satires of the second book he seems to have shed his Epicureanism. He does not indeed commit himself to Stoicism; he puts his expositions of the paradoxes in the mouths of others, Damasippus and Davus, and leaves his readers guessing how far he accepts them himself.[9] He certainly seems to have felt there was something in them, otherwise he would hardly have devoted over three hundred lines to an exposition of the Stoic view that all are mad save the *sapiens*.[10] There is, of course, something faintly ridiculous about Damasippus the ruined art dealer and his philosophic doctor Stertinius, but why not leave them alone? Ridicule may be the prelude to conversion, and it would not have been surprising to see the uneasy mixture of interest and amusement displayed in this satire developing into whole-hearted adherence, if the author were not Horace. For Horace was not one of nature's converts.

In one of his Odes Horace describes how, having neglected the gods while following philosophy, he was forced to return to old ways by witnessing thunder in a clear sky.[11] This phenomenon was inconsistent with the materialistic explanations of thunder given by the Epicureans, and it seems clear that Horace wished to proclaim his abandonment of the creed of his youth. How much importance we should attach to this 'conversion' is hard to say; it is probable that Horace's Epicureanism had already been to all intents and purposes left behind when he wrote this Ode. It is only in the loose and

* For I have learned that the gods live a life free from care.

popular sense that the Horace of the Odes can be called an Epicurean. There is nothing of the distinctive Epicurean doctrines in the Odes, and much that is un-Epicurean; the respect for traditional religion, the use of mythology and the appeal to patriotism are either inconsistent with Epicureanism or alien to its spirit. On the other hand we cannot speak of a conversion to Stoicism. The phenomenon of thunder in a clear sky leads not to the Stoic belief in a rational world order, but to the popular cult of Fortuna. Many of the Odes are consistent with Stoic teaching, but it is not often that we can point to anything that bears the distinctive mark of the Stoa.[12]

When we turn to the *Epistles* we find Horace detached and inconsistent, susceptible at times to the claims of philosophy, but unwilling to give himself to any one school. He calls himself in one place a 'pig from Epicurus's stye', but this is not to be taken as a serious profession of faith. Epicureanism has in fact receded into the background. The choice is rather between Aristippus and the Stoa.

> *nunc agilis fio et mersor civilibus undis*
> *virtutis verae custos rigidusque satelles;*
> *nunc in Aristippi furtim praecepta relabor*
> *et mihi res non me rebus subiungere conor.* *[13]

Aristippus is the philosopher for the man of the world, and Horace is a man of the world. But not consistently so; seriousness keeps breaking in, and then it is to the Stoics that he turns. The paradoxes continue to haunt him, though he still cannot quite accept them:

> *ad summam, sapiens uno minor est Iove, dives,*
> *liber, honoratus, pulcher, rex denique regum,*
> *praecipue sanus, nisi cum pituita molesta est.*†[14]

---

* Now, all alert I cope with life's rough main,
  A loyal follower in true virtue's train.
  Anon to Aristippus's camp I flit,
  And say, the world's for me, not I for it. (CONINGTON)

† So to sum up: the sage is half divine,
  Rich, free, great, handsome, king of kings, in fine;
  A miracle of health from toe to crown,
  Mind, heart and head, save when his nose runs down. (CONINGTON)

Horace cannot resist the joke at the end. The humourless earnestness of the Stoic is out of keeping with Horace's own character and that of his *sermones*. Yet in one at least of the *Epistles* he preaches Stoicism with every appearance of conviction, when he reinterprets a scene from Euripides's *Bacchae* in a moral sense. The truly good and wise man will be unmoved by Pentheus's threats. Pentheus may take from him all his goods and put him in chains, but this will matter nothing to him. God will release him; that is, in true Stoic spirit, he will assert his independence by taking his life.[15]

Virgil wrote no *sermones,* and it is not so easy to follow the development of his thought as it is in the case of Horace. But we know that he studied in his youth under the Epicurean Siro, and we have in the *Catalepton* a poem attributed to him in which he looks forward in true Epicurean spirit to freeing life from all care: *vitamque ab omni vindicabimus cura.*[16] It is clear too from the frequent verbal echoes of Lucretius in his works that the *De Rerum Natura* made a powerful impression on him. But he later moved away from Siro and Lucretius. There was no sudden, abrupt conversion; that was not Virgil's way. *Felix qui potuit rerum cognoscere causas.*[17] Lucretius, whom Virgil surely had in mind when he wrote this line, was *felix,* even though Virgil's own approach to nature was different. Something of his Epicurean upbringing survives in the *Georgics.* In the first book, after giving a list of the various signs by which birds foretell the weather, he goes on to say that this is not because they have foreknowledge implanted by heaven; it can be explained by purely natural causes.[18] His explanation, with its Lucretian phraseology, is in the Epicurean tradition. On the other hand in the fourth book he gives, though without actually associating himself with the view, the Stoic theory that there is a portion of the divine in everything;[19] and on one important question, the growth of civilization, he definitely rejects the Epicurean point of view :

> *ante Iovem nulli subigebant arva coloni;*
> *ne signare quidem aut partiri limite campum*

*fas erat: in medium quaerebant, ipsaque tellus
omnia liberius nullo poscente ferebat.*[20]

Here we have the old idea, quite alien to Epicureanism, of the Golden Age, when earth bore everything freely. Virgil has abandoned the Lucretian theory of the gradual rise of man. Yet even in this passage a trace of Epicureanism can be detected. Jupiter, according to Virgil, brought an end to the Golden Age *ut varias usus meditando extunderet artes.*†[21] In Virgil's picture there is still room for a gradual learning by experience.

The *Aeneid* shows Virgil to have moved still further away from Epicureanism. To some extent he has moved in the direction of Stoicism. There is Stoic influence in Anchises's exposition of the nature of the universe and the destiny of the human soul in Book VI, though Stoicism is combined with ideas of purification and reincarnation which belong rather to Orphism and Pythagoreanism; there are hints of Stoicism in the way the character of Aeneas is depicted; and the idea of fate which pervades the work owes something to Stoic theories. But whether Stoic or not—and it would be a mistake to over-emphasize the Stoic element—the *Aeneid* is certainly not Epicurean. The sixth book, not to mention any other part of the work—is contrary to all that Epicurus taught. *Rursus in antiquas referuntur religiones* might well have been Lucretius's comment.

Enough has been said to show that Epicureanism suffered a remarkable decline at Rome in the years following the extinction of the Republic. How are we to account for this? The most obvious answer would be that it was out of keeping with the new age. Apart from the fact that Augustus had had a Stoic master, his whole programme of moral and religious revival was incompatible with Epicurean materialism. In this environment an Epicurean might well think it prudent to keep quiet, if he was not forced by the pressure of official propaganda or public

---

* Before Jove's time no settlers brought the land under subjection;
  Not lawful even to divide the plain with landmarks and boundaries.
  All produce went to a common pool, and earth unprompted
  Was free with all her fruits. (C. DAY LEWIS)
  † So thought and experiment might forge man's various crafts. (C. DAY LEWIS)

opinion to change his mind. Yet the obvious answer is not necessarily the right one. In other circumstances Epicureans could stick to their views, and the fact that a certain Lucius Varus is recorded to have been both an Epicurean and a friend of Augustus suggests that there was tolerance in high places.[22] It would perhaps be truer to say that the establishment of the Augustan peace made Epicureanism seem irrelevant. *Deus nobis haec otia fecit.* Lucretius had hailed Epicurus as *deus—deus ille fuit deus, optime Memmi*—and *otium* was an Epicurean ideal. Augustus was a more effective god than the remote sage of Athens,[23] and the *otium* he established more real than the peace of the Epicurean garden, which might well be disturbed by political insecurity. Varius, Virgil's friend, an Epicurean to begin with and author of a poem, probably Lucretian in spirit, on Death, ended by using his poetical talents in praise of Augustus.[24]

Along with the decline of Epicureanism there went a general decline of interest in speculation and a concentration on the moral aspect of philosophy. Philosophy in Cicero's day wore a twofold aspect; it provided an explanation of life and a guide to life. It was at once philosophy (in the modern sense) and religion. In the Augustan age the latter aspect predominates; the preacher ousts the professor. The ideal of the intellectual search for truth grows weaker. There were still those who felt the desire to know the causes of things, but whether through despair at reaching certainty or the feeling that there were other things more important, they could do no more than express the desire and leave it at that. Propertius looks forward to spending his old age in studying nature; but though he expends twenty-two lines on the various physical and philosophical questions to which he proposes to devote himself when he is too old for love, it is permissible to doubt whether he ever did so occupy himself. Virgil too gives noble expression to the ideal of the philosophic poet who understands and explains nature:

> me vero primum dulces ante omnia Musae,
> quarum sacra fero ingenti percussus amore,
> accipiant caelique vias et sidera monstrent,
> defectus solis varios lunaeque labores;

unde tremor terris, qua vi maria alta tumescant
obicibus ruptis rursusque in se ipsa residant,
quid tantum Oceano properent se tingere soles
*hiberni, vel quae tardis mora noctibus obstet.**

But, he goes on, he himself is not capable of rising to such heights; he is content to look at the rivers and the woods and to enjoy without understanding.[25]

But if few of the Augustans were interested in the true, many were interested in the good. *Vis recte vivere, quis non?* says Horace;[26] and his own *Satires* and *Epistles* show how much he and his age were concerned with the problem how to live aright. There was no lack of preachers to point the way to the good life. The Stoics and their allies the Cynics repeated their message with what seems to us a wearisome monotony. The ills against which they inveighed were avarice, ambition, luxury, restlessness and discontent; their ideal was moral self-sufficiency, to be free from the domination of desires and passions, content with a little and armed to meet all the blows of fortune. Horace, for all his detachment and his occasional ridicule of the moralists, was evidently impressed by their teaching, and such ideas frequently recur in his writing. The greater part of mankind, he says, suffer from avarice and ambition. Men go on making money, never content with what they have, always wanting more. If you make wealth and success your aim, you will become too much attached to them, and if you lose them, you will have lost everything; if you are too much pleased with success, you will feel the shock of failure more. If money is not one's slave, it becomes one's master.[27] So too with the passions; they prevent one from being a free man. They are moreover unhealthy states of mind, or forms of madness; the ideal is to be healthy and sane mentally as well as physically. So let us free ourselves from anger, desire and fear, curing

* Since Poetry for me comes first—my goddess and chief delight
  Whose devotee I am, with a master-passion adoring—
  I wish above all she accept me, revealing the stars and the sky-routes,
  The several eclipses of the sun, the moon pallid in labour,
  The cause of earthquakes and the force that compels the deep sea
  To swell, to break all bounds, to fall back on itself again;
  The reason why winter suns race on to dip in the ocean,
  And what delays the long nights. (C. DAY LEWIS)

ourselves by waking up early in the morning and reading philosophy.[28]

Such moralizing, though no doubt sincere and not without pertinence and force in any age, was mainly derivative, and where he dwells on such themes Horace has little to add to the preaching of countless moralists but his wit and epigrammatic brevity. There is more to attract in those parts of his writing where he is more personal and more original. He had throughout his life, derived perhaps from the Epicureanism of his early years, a keen feeling for friendship and personal relations, which the Stoic and Cynic preachers had not. There are times when he forgets to be a philosopher and writes on human relations with the easy tact and urbane common sense of the man of the world; we find him turning against the Cynics, who made a virtue of poverty and squalor, and interpreting *virtus* in a manner that the Stoics would hardly have approved:

> *aut virtus nomen inane est*
> *aut decus et pretium recte petit experiens vir.**[29]

In one of his early satires he discourses in Epicurean spirit on forgiveness and tolerance to the faults of friends.[30] Such teaching was later thrust into the background by the sterner moralizing of the opposite school, which laid more stress on independence than on friendship, and had little use, in theory at any rate, for tolerance or forgiveness. In Horace's last utterance on conduct, however, forgiveness is mentioned once more:

> *non es avarus: abi. quid cetera, iam simul isto*
> *cum vitio fugere? caret tibi pectus inani*
> *ambitione? caret mortis formidine et ira?*
> *somnia terrores magicos miracula sagas*
> *nocturnos lemures portentaque Thessala rides?*
> *natales grate numeras? ignoscis amicis?*
> *lenior et melior fis accedente senecta?*†[31]

---

* If Virtue's aught beyond an empty Name,
 Rewards and Honours they with Justice claim.
                                    (PHILIP FRANCIS)

† You are not covetous: be satisfied.
 But are you tainted with no Vice beside?
 From vain Ambition, Dread of Death's Decree,
 And fell Resentment, is thy Bosom free?

The lines have at first a Stoic-Cynic ring, with their familiar diagnosis of avarice and ambition as the great ills of mankind; but freedom from fear of death and contempt of magic, ghosts and the like suggest rather Epicureanism. Numbering one's birthdays gratefully recalls the Cynic sermons against discontent, but forgiveness of one's friends, as suggested above, is rather an Epicurean theme. We see how Epicurean teaching could merge with Stoic to provide a morality free from dogma for the ordinary sensitive man who wished to live a good life.

Horace belonged to the older generation of Augustans who grew up at the end of the Republic. He had his education at the time when Cicero's philosophical works were coming out, and studied in Cicero's own school, the Academy. Thus he carried into the Augustan age something of the intellectual interests of the Republic. For the younger generation, those whose habits of thought were formed when the Republic was already a thing of the past, there was little stimulus to intellectual curiosity. The men of Ovid's generation grew up in an environment more or less indifferent to philosophy. We know from the elder Seneca how they were educated. It was an education in rhetoric, not the broad general education that Cicero had advocated, in which eloquence was to be nurtured by philosophy, law and history, but a narrow training in self-expression, in which philosophy has shrunk to a few commonplaces. One of the most famous of the Augustan rhetoricians, Porcius Latro, used to compose *sententiae* on such themes as fortune, cruelty, the evils of the age and the contempt of riches, which could be used equally well in any declamation. These he would call *supellex,* furniture. Other rhetoricians used philosophical matter for more extended disquisitions, but these *loci philosophoumeni* were just as much furniture, not part of

---

Say, can you laugh indignant at the Schemes
Of magic Terrours, visionary Dreams,
Portentous Wonders, witching Imps of Hell,
The nightly Goblin and enchanting Spell?
Dost thou recount with Gratitude and Mirth
The Day revolv'd that gave thy Being birth?
Indulge the Failings of thy Friends, and grow
More mild and virtuous, as the Seasons flow?

(PHILIP FRANCIS)

the structure, but more or less irrelevant adornments.[32] There was no background of thought or knowledge, and no interest in ideas except so far as they contributed to the effectiveness of the declamation.

Ovid had his education in the rhetorical schools described by Seneca, and although he proceeded to Athens, philosophy seems to have played little part in his education. He could pick up such ideas as were going about and use them, as in Pythagoras's discourse in the last book of the *Metamorphoses*, but he does not give the impression of having thought or felt deeply on philosophical matters. Pythagoras is made to preach vegetarianism, but it is unlikely that Ovid was ever tempted to take it up, as the younger Seneca did for a time.[33] There is no trace of the consolations of philosophy in the *Tristia* and *Letters from Pontus*.

> *Gratia, Musa, tibi. nam tu solatia praebes;*
> *tu curae requies, tu medicina mali.*[*][34]

It is the Muse who supplies solace and relief. Philosophy, the professed physician of the mind, did not fail Ovid; she was not even summoned to the bedside.

Meantime, though one would not guess it from Ovid, the philosophers had been actively teaching in Rome, and one of them, Sextius, had for a time a considerable following. He was a Stoic, says Seneca, from whom we learn most of what we know about him, though he did not call himself one, and he preached a heroic morality of spiritual struggle. He saw life as a battle, a battle against folly, with the wise man prepared against every attack. He did not argue; he inspired. 'What power and spirit he has', exclaims Seneca. 'Others instruct, argue, quibble, but do not inspire you, because they are not inspired themselves. But when you read Sextius you will say: "He is alive, active, free, greater than human. He sends me away filled with a mighty confidence." '[35]

The old idea of philosophy as an intellectual discipline has faded; men now look to the philosophers for something that

---

* Thine, Muse, the gift. From thee doth comfort flow,
Thou bringst relief and healing to my woe.

makes them feel better and stronger. Moreover philosophy now asks of them a whole-hearted allegiance. In the time of Cicero and Cato philosophical study could be united with literary culture and political activity. Now it demanded the abandonment of old pursuits. Sextius gave up a political career for philosophy; Crassitius, who had made a reputation as a scholar with his commentary on Cinna's *Smyrna,* suddenly gave up teaching and became a follower of Sextius.[36] The sudden change, the abandonment of former pursuits, show philosophy as a religion exacting and exclusive in its demands.

RELIGION IN THE AUGUSTAN AGE

WHILE PHILOSOPHY declined in the Augustan age, religion revived, fostered and promoted by the Princeps, with the support of the leading writers of the day. Temples were restored; old priesthoods were revived and given new prestige; the Vestal Virgins had their dignity enhanced. The whole apparatus of the state religion was set in order and restored to its old position in public life.

The policy was in keeping with the conservatism of Augustus and his desire to foster patriotism and national spirit. Roman religion was intimately bound up with Roman public life, and the old belief that the welfare of the state depended on the due performance of the rites and ceremonies, a belief which had not died out even in the later Republic, made it natural that once the new regime was established the restoration of religion should be a part of its programme. The evils of the civil wars might well seem a punishment for the neglect of the gods, and a return to old ways the surest means of providing for the survival and welfare of Rome and of her Empire.

While in the main Augustus aimed at reviving the old Roman state religion he was not narrowly nationalistic in religious matters. 'Such foreign rites as were ancient and well established he observed with great respect; the rest he held in contempt.'[1] He discouraged exotic oriental cults, but approved the old and respectable gods of Greece which had long been assimilated to Roman religion. In the description of Aeneas's shield in the eighth book of the *Aeneid* Virgil includes a picture of the battle of Actium. On one side is Augustus with the gods of Rome, on the other Antonius and his Egyptian queen, and with them dog-headed Anubis and other monstrous oriental deities. Apollo of Actium decides the issue and puts to flight the eastern deities. It is a conflict between east and west, between civilization and barbarism, and Apollo is on the side of civilization.

Apollo was essentially a Greek god, but it was he whom Augustus chose as his peculiar patron. When he wished to add to the existing cults a new cult especially associated with himself and his new regime he erected the magnificent new temple of Apollo on the Palatine. This was more than a private temple, as the Princeps was more than a private citizen. It was incorporated into the state worship. The Sibylline books were transferred there from the temple of Jupiter Capitolinus, and when the great secular games of 17 B.C. were held, the new religious centre on the Palatine had an equal place in the celebrations with the old centre on the Capitol, and in Horace's hymn Augustus's patron deity has pride of place.

Thus while linking up his age with the religious traditions of the past, Augustus by judicious innovation gave it a religious stamp peculiar to itself. At the same time he closely associated his own person with the religions of Rome. He became *pontifex maximus* and member of all important priestly colleges. New temples to Divus Julius, Mars Ultor and Apollo of Actium honoured the adopted son and avenger of Caesar and the victor of Actium; and though in Rome Augustus might decline divine honours, such acts as the deification of his adoptive father, the conferment of the majestic title of Augustus and the institution of the worship of the *genius Augusti* set him above ordinary humanity and introduced a new element into the complex of cults and sentiment which made up Roman religion.

The two greatest poets of the Augustan age, both of them closely in touch with Augustus through Maecenas, were in sympathy with his religious policy, and in different ways helped to further it. Horace preaches the restoration of temples, attributes the ills of Rome to neglect of religion and reminds the Romans that they owe their Empire to submission to the gods.[2] And that Horace is here not merely the dutiful exponent of official policy is shown by some lines in one of the satires, written before Augustus set on foot the restoration of temples;

in words which have every appearance of expressing his private and personal feelings Horace urges the rich to spend money on their country rather than on themselves, and asks: 'Why do the ancient temples of the gods fall into ruin?'[3]

Virgil supported the revival of religion less directly than Horace, but none the less effectively. The *Aeneid* gives abundant evidence of his sympathy with the various aspects of contemporary religion, and his conviction that the establishment of Augustus as ruler of the Roman world was in accordance with the will of the gods. The history of the Roman people, culminating in Augustus, is, no less than its origin, the fulfilment of the divine will, and it is Jupiter who, near the beginning of the poem, announces that he has given the Romans an empire without limit.[4]

As regards the person of Augustus himself, the two poets readily ascribe to him divinity, whether present or future. Virgil, who at the time of the triumvirate had hailed him as *deus*, invokes him at the beginning of the *Georgics* and pictures him as destined for divinity, while Jupiter in the first book of the *Aeneid* promises to Venus that she will receive her descendant into heaven and that he will be the object of men's prayers.[5] Horace, in an ode probably written at the end of 28 B.C., calls upon Mercury to descend to earth in the form of Augustus. In a later ode he pictures him drinking nectar in the company of Pollux and Hercules, heroes who have won divinity by their strength of purpose, while elsewhere he announces that he will be held to be a *praesens divus* when he has added the Britons and Parthians to the Roman empire.[6] The precise significance of the different forms of divinity ascribed to, or foretold for, the Princeps does not concern us here; it is enough to note that Virgil and Horace, and presumably the public for which they wrote, had no difficulty in accepting the idea of the divinity of the Princeps, and were indeed inclined to go further than Augustus himself in this respect.

The religion of the farm and the countryside was not, as was that of the Roman state, the object of official encouragement. The sympathies of the Augustans were, however, naturally drawn towards these ancient cults, so closely woven into the life of the countryside. They appealed to the antiquarianism of the new age, its belief in ancient loyalties and in the virtues of a simple peasantry. *Sacra deum* belong to the country no less than *exiguo assueta iuventus*,[7] and the rites of the countryside had all the stronger appeal perhaps now that the traditional life of the farmer was threatened by the growth of large estates run by slave labour.

Such a sentiment was hardly to be found in the previous age. Lucretius had no more use for the gods of the countryside than for the Olympians. Goat-footed satyrs, nymphs and fauns, Pan with his pipe, were merely inventions of the countryman who peopled deserted places with inhabitants because he could not bear to feel lonely.[8] It is significant that Virgil, proclaiming his love of the country, probably in conscious opposition to Lucretius, expresses it in terms of religion:

> *fortunatus et ille deos qui novit agrestes*
> *Panaque Silvanumque senem Nymphasque sorores,*[*][9]

those very deities whom Lucretius had emphatically rejected.

Thus Virgil, addressing the countryman in the *Georgics*, advises him above all to observe the worship of the gods and to carry out the annual rites of Ceres:

> *cuncta tibi Cererem pubes agrestis adoret:*
> *cui tu lacte favos et miti dilue Baccho,*
> *terque novas circum felix eat hostia fruges*
> *omnis quam chorus et socii comitentur ovantes,*
> *et Cererem clamore vocent in tecta; neque ante*
> *falcem maturis quisquam supponat aristis*
> *quam Cereri torta redimitus tempora quercu*
> *det motus incompositos et carmina dicat.*[†][10]

* Yet he also is fortunate who knows
  The rustic deities, both Pan and that old
  Silvanus, and the sisterhood of the nymphs.
                                    (R. C. TREVELYAN)
† Let all your rustic youth now worship Ceres:
  For her in milk and soft wine you must drench
  The honeycomb and the auspicious victim
  Must be led three times round the growing crops,
  Followed by the whole chorus of your fellows
  With loud exulting cries summoning Ceres
  To dwell within their homes. And let none put

Horace too writes sympathetically of the countrywoman
Phidyle with her simple offering to the *lares* and *penates*, of the
sacrifice of a kid to the fountain of Bandusia, of Faunus and
his annual festival when all make holiday.[11] Tibullus likes to
picture himself as a countryman, and is careful to include in
his picture the farmer's ritual acts of worship as well as his
work, to describe how he makes an act of worship where a tree
trunk or ancient stone bears its wreath of flowers, offers a wreath
to Ceres, sets Priapus to watch over the fields, sacrifices a lamb
to the lares and sprinkles Pales with milk.[12] Elsewhere he gives
a detailed and charming picture of the festival of the Ambar-
valia. Ritual purity must be observed, hands and clothes be
clean. The procession proceeds round the farm, led by the
sacrificial lamb, with prayers for the wellbeing of the crops,
and the ceremony ends with drinking and merrymaking.[13] It
is a holy day which is also a holiday. *Rura cano rurisque deos.*[14]
Tibullus sings of the country and the country's gods; for him
as for Virgil religion was an essential part of country life.

By the side of these country gods that appealed so strongly
to Roman sentiment the Greek gods and goddesses, the deities
of mythology and art, might seem remote and unreal, figures
whose appeal was aesthetic rather than religious. Yet an
educated man might well feel a more personal sympathy with
the gods of Greece, rich as they were in associations and
symbolism, than in the impersonal spirits of the countryside,
who had no meaning apart from the life and activities over
which they presided. So when Horace prays to Apollo it is the
prayer of a poet to the god of poetry, the expression of his
personal desires and aspirations. For Mercury he had a special
sympathy, and to him he addresses a hymn which, though
devoid of personal reference, is beautiful and moving. Bacchus
is for Horace a symbol both of poetical inspiration to be
accepted joyfully and of the wilder instincts of man, to be kept
under control, a power to inspire conflicting emotions, joy and
fear combined, and surely a very real power to Horace.[15]

> His sickle to the ripe corn, till, his brows
> With oak-wreath crowned, he has flung artless gambols
> And sung his harvest hymns in Ceres' honour.
>   (R. C. TREVELYAN)

The Augustan poets were of course at home in the whole field of Greek mythology. The myths had come to Rome with the literature in which they were enshrined, and in the late Republic in particular the influence of Alexandria had made a knowledge of mythology an essential part of the poet's equipment. This type of learning became something of a fashion with the *poetae novi* of Cicero's day, and the fashion continued into the succeeding age. Propertius with his numerous mythological allusions is very much in the Alexandrian tradition. Generally speaking, Greek mythology was for the Romans what it had been to the Alexandrians and was to be to many writers of modern Europe, a storehouse of charming and beautiful stories. But some at any rate of the myths had been more than this; they had been in origin attempts to explain the world and mankind, and even after the development of philosophical and scientific explanation they could still be used to provide an interpretation of life. And they were on occasion so used by the Augustans.

The poet, says Socrates in the *Phaedo*,[16] uses myth rather than rational argument (μύθους ἀλλ᾽ οὐ λόγους), and it is not surprising that the Augustan poets should follow this tradition. Yet Lucretius had preferred λόγος to μῦθος and Virgil and Horace grew up under his influence or that of his school, so that it is not without significance that they chose a different method from his. We can observe the change of outlook in the question of the origin of mankind and of society. In one of his early works Horace gives an outline of the Epicurean theory; man was born from the earth and was a *mutum et turpe pecus,* quarrelsome and barbarous, until laws were established from fear of wrongdoing.[17] Later we find that he has abandoned this rationalist view and resorted to mythology; in the *Odes* it is Prometheus who creates the first man and Mercury who teaches the arts of civilization.[18] Virgil too in his early years presumably accepted the Epicurean anthropology. But, as we have seen already, he deliberately abandoned it and returned to the old Greek idea of the Golden Age. He did not, however, simply take over the myth in its commonly accepted form; he gave it a new interpretation of his own. According to Hesiod's version there had been four ages associated with different metals, gold, silver, bronze and iron, and apart from the age of the heroes, inserted after that of bronze, it is a straightforward story of degeneration, the latest age being the worst. In Virgil's version in the *Georgics* the age of Saturn, when the earth bore all things freely, was succeeded by the age of Jupiter, when men had to work for their living, and, what is the important point, there was purpose in the change. Jupiter himself willed that the way of husbandry should not be an easy one; he did not wish his realm to stagnate in ease and sloth.[19] Here we have a serious and creative use of myth as a means to explain the nature of human life.

A further reinterpretation of the same myth is to be found in the *Aeneid*. In the eighth book Evander explains to Aeneas that the earliest inhabitants of the site of Rome were Fauns and Nymphs and savage men without knowledge of agriculture. Then came the reign of Saturn, who taught men civilization and laws; this was the Golden Age, an age of peace, which was followed by a worse age of strife and self seeking.[20] Here we find a striking departure from the version of the *Georgics*; now there is an era of savagery preceding the Golden Age and the latter comes after, not before, the development of civilization. The new version fits in with the theme of the *Aeneid*, which is the foundation of a state, and with the hope of a golden age to be reborn with Augustus. If the founding of the Roman people was the expression of the divine will and the Augustan age was a new Golden Age, then the reign of Saturn, the original Golden Age, cannot be what it was in the *Georgics*; it must be an age of law and civilization. Virgil's thought has developed, and in the absence of any religious or scientific orthodoxy he had no difficulty in adapting his account of the origins of society to fit his new point of view.

The greatest of Virgilian myths, using the word in its widest sense, is the account of the Underworld in Book VI of the *Aeneid*. The idea no doubt came from the *Odyssey*, but the episode has much greater significance than Homer's Νέκυια. In Latin literature there was a partial precedent in Cicero, who in the *Somnium Scipionis*, as we have seen, followed the

Platonic method of exposition by myth rather than by rational argument, and used the myth to convey his conviction of the survival of the soul after death. But Virgil goes farther than Cicero; by placing the home of the souls in the underworld he deliberately turns his back on the philosophers, and on Cicero's picture of a remote region among the stars, and returns to an older and more popular tradition. Moreover Cicero, while accepting the survival of the soul and depicting the happy future destined for the good, had excluded the punishment of the bad from his picture, and elsewhere dismissed the old stories of such punishments as old wives' fables. Virgil on the other hand includes the punishments of Tartarus, along with much else that philosophy would have rejected.

Augustus did for Roman religion what could be done by official action. He restored the state religion and gave it a secure place in Roman life, which it continued to hold until it gave way before the onslaughts of Christianity. The old rites continued to be performed, and the old feeling that the welfare of Rome was bound up with the worship of her gods was still alive in the fourth century. So far as Augustus's acts were responsible for this, his revival of religion may be called a success. But the state religion was a formal affair, a matter of ritual and cult, expressing the needs of the community rather than of the individual. It could not satisfy the emotions or the intellect or the moral aspirations of the individual, and what they could not find in the state religion men found in philosophy, or in those eastern religions which Augustus had frowned upon. Jupiter of the Capitol might still serve as the symbol of Roman power, might still be invoked as protector and preserver of the Empire, but the ordinary subject of Rome turned to other deities for help in his daily life. Already in the time of Augustus Isis was a favourite object of feminine devotion, and not many years after the gods of Egypt had been put to flight at Actium we find Ovid appealing to those very gods, including the dog-headed Anubis, to come to the aid of his mistress.[21] The religion of the countryside was no doubt practised as before, but in the post-Augustan period it ceased to attract men of letters as it had attracted Virgil and Tibullus. In the time

of Persius, in the mid-first century A.D., poets who sang of
country life on Augustan lines ('with baskets, hearth, pigs, the
festival of Pales with smoking hay, whence came Remus . . .')
were a fit object of satire.[22] In view of the provincial origin of
so many of the intellectual leaders of the Empire it is hardly
surprising that they should have been little interested in a
religion that was purely Italian.

The sentiment which inspired or was stimulated by
Augustus's religious policy was comparatively short-lived. It
affected men of the generation of Virgil and Horace who had
known the despair of the period of civil war and shared in the
hopes aroused by Actium. It had little effect on the younger
generation who grew up when the memory of the period before
Actium was growing faint. Ovid's attitude to religion seems to
be one of polite indifference. For him it is something which
should be kept up for its social uses.

> expedit esse deos, et, ut expedit, esse putemus;
> dentur in antiquos tura merumque focos.

There follow lines which read by themselves give the impression
of an enlightened piety:

> nec secura quies illos similisque sopori
> detinet; innocue vivite; numen adest.
> reddite depositum: pietas sua foedera servet:
> fraus absit: vacuas caedis habete manus.

But the conclusion forbids us to take the poet too seriously:

> ludite, si sapitis, solas impune puellas:
> hac minus est una fraude tuenda fides.*[23]

The poet of the *Ars Amatoria,* from which these lines come,
was also the poet of the *Fasti,* with its detailed accounts of the
various religious ceremonies of the Roman year. Ovid writes

---

* Religion's useful; so, let us believe,
  And to the gods their usual offerings give.
  They do not sleep in quiet negligence;
  Their godhead's nigh. So live without offence.
  Keep faith; observe the bonds of loyalty;
  Deceive not; let your hands from blood be free.
  Women alone, if wise, you'll safely cheat;
  You may allow yourself this one deceit.

of these with some sympathy and understanding, but leaves one with the impression that he was not altogether happy in his choice of subject. The *Fasti* remains a sign of his virtuosity and a tribute to the prevailing fashion of antiquarianism rather than the expression of a genuine feeling for Roman traditions. Aetiological poetry of this sort hardly implies a lively religious feeling. It had originated in Alexandria, when the old legends and rites had ceased to be part of a living tradition and had become rather the object of an interested curiosity.

If we may judge by the success of the *Metamorphoses* in comparison with the *Fasti*, Greek mythology made a greater appeal to Ovid than Roman traditions. We do not, however, find that he makes any attempt to use the myths to explain or illuminate human life; he takes them as he finds them and adds nothing in the way of interpretation. He adopts the traditional account of the successive stages of decline from the Golden through the Silver and Bronze ages to the Age of Iron; his version is a neat summing up of the Greek tradition, with no attempt such as we find in Virgil to reinterpret or give meaning to the myth. Indeed he robs it of much of its point by introducing shortly afterwards the myth of man's second creation after the flood from the stones thrown by Deucalion. Virgil had touched on this story in the *Georgics,* but did not treat it seriously or at length.[24] Ovid, undeterred by its lack of significance and attracted by its picturesque possibilities, tells it at length. One is left with the feeling that for him the myths concerning the origin of mankind were no more than stories.

At the end of the *Metamorphoses* Ovid prays to the gods of Rome that the day may be long delayed when Augustus leaves the earth for heaven:

> *di, precor, Aeneae comites, quibus ensis et ignis*
> *cesserunt, dique indigites genitorque Quirine*
> *urbis et invicti genitor Gradive Quirini*
> *Vestaque Caesareos inter sacrata Penates*
> *et cum Caesarea tu, Phoebe domestice, Vesta,*
> *quique tenes altus Tarpeias Iupiter arces*
> *quosque alios vati fas appellare piumque est:*

> *tarda sit illa dies et nostro serior aevo*
> *qua caput Augustum quem temperat orbe relicto*
> *accedat caelo faveatque precantibus absens.**25

The lines recall Virgil's appeal to the same gods towards the
end of the first book of the *Georgics*:

> *di patrii, Indigetes, et Romule Vestaque mater*
> *quae Tuscum Tiberim et Romana Palatia servas*
> *hunc saltem everso iuvenem succurrere saeclo*
> *ne prohibete.*†26

Some thirty years have intervened between Virgil's words and
those of Ovid. Augustus is no longer the young man to whom
men's eyes turn as the saviour of a stricken age, but the
accepted ruler. The heartfelt cry has changed to a pious formula;
the *di indigetes*, Romulus and Vesta, are no longer symbols of
a deep and newly found feeling for Roman traditions, but
merely the gods whom it is right and proper for the poet to
address.

> * Celestials, who for Rome your cares employ;
> Ye gods, who guarded the remains of Troy;
> Ye native gods, here born and fix'd by fate;
> Quirinus, founder of the Roman state;
> O parent Mars, from whom Quirinus sprung;
> Chaste Vesta, Caesar's household gods among
> Most sacred held; domestic Phoebus, thou
> To whom with Vesta chaste alike we bow;
> Great guardian of the high Tarpeian rock;
> And all ye powers whom poets may invoke;
> O grant, that day may claim our sorrows late,
> When lov'd Augustus shall submit to fate,
> Visit those seats where gods and heroes dwell,
> And leave, in tears, the world he rul'd so well.
> (LEONARD WELSTED)
>
> † Gods of my country, heroes of this land,
> Yea and thou, Romulus, thou, mother Vesta,
> Who Tuscan Tiber and Roman Palatine
> Keepest in holy ward, at least vouchsafe
> That this our prince uplift our prostrate age.
> (L. A S. JERMYN)

VIII

THE NATIONAL SPIRIT

'WE WERE like foreigners, strangers wandering in our own city, when your books led us home and enabled us at last to recognize who we were and where we lived. You have revealed the age of our country, the chronology of our history, the rules of our religion and our priesthoods, our practices at home and in the field, our topography and the names, classification, functions and origins of everything sacred and secular.'[1] These words of Cicero addressed to Varro give a striking indication of the hellenization of Roman culture at the end of the Republic. Cicero perhaps exaggerates, for he himself at any rate was well acquainted with Roman history, delighted in the study of Roman law and proclaimed the virtues of the Latin language and the general superiority of Rome to Greece.[2] But on the whole it was no doubt true that the mind of the Romans of his age was formed on Greek literature and Greek thought, and Roman traditions were the object of indifference and even in some cases of contempt, that *insolens domesticarum rerum fastidium* of which Cicero spoke elsewhere.[3] It was very different in the Augustan age. The researches of Varro bore fruit in a new interest in Roman history and antiquities and a new feeling for the Italian countryside. There is a new consciousness of nationality, and a new relationship between literature and government; the writers now identify themselves closely with imperial policy and make it their business to foster a national and patriotic spirit. This sentiment is most marked in the writers of Maecenas's circle; it pervades the mature work of Virgil, forms an important element in the *Odes* of Horace, and even affects to some degree the work of Propertius.

Virgil's earliest work has little of this spirit. The *Eclogues* take us into a pastoral world, charming and irresponsible, placed in a setting which seems to be now Sicily, now Italy, now a purely imaginary landscape. But in the years after Philippi it was impossible to escape altogether, and the harsh realities of the day intrude even on Virgil's Arcadia. The evicted farmer must leave his home:

> nos patriae fines et dulcia linquimus arva,
> nos patriam fugimus . . .
> impius haec tam culta novalia miles habebit,
> barbarus has segetes: en quo discordia cives
> producit miseros.*⁴

But it is only indirectly and in allegory that Virgil depicts the plight of Italy under the triumvirs. And in the fourth *Eclogue,* where he expresses his hopes for the future, he uses the imagery of the mythical Golden Age to produce a poem which, although inspired by the consulship of Pollio, seems strangely irrelevant to the actual historical circumstances of the year 40 B.C.

The *Georgics* are very different in tone from the *Eclogues.* Written at the suggestion of Maecenas and opening with an invocation of Octavian, the poem shows that the author has ceased to speak in allegories and has come out into the open politically. It shows too that he has moved from Arcadia into a world closer to reality, that of agriculture and hard work. The close of the first book, with its sombre picture of a world at war and agriculture neglected, seems to reflect the gloom of the years before Actium; the serene and happy spirit of the second book, even apart from a specific reference to contemporary events,⁵ shows that the victory of Actium has brought new hope. This book includes an eloquent passage, inspired perhaps by Varro, in praise of Italy as a land of unequalled richness and fertility.⁶ In the picture are included the ancient cities, the lakes and even, in the passage on the Julian harbour, contemporary public works; and the passage ends with a reference to the

*   I from my sweet fields
And home's familiar bound even now depart.
Exiled from home am I.
            These fallows, trimmed so fair,
Some brutal soldier will possess, these fields
An alien master. Ah! to what a pass
Has civil discord brought our hapless folk!
                (JAMES RHOADES)

martial races of Italy and the heroes of Roman history, including Octavian himself. The pattern of Augustan sentiment becomes clear; Italian patriotism, a return to the sturdy peasant virtues, a pride in Rome's history and a loyal support of her latest hero, the Princeps himself. At the end of the second book the national note is sounded once more; the generalized picture of the peace and simplicity of country life ends with a specific reference to this life as having bred the men who made Rome great:

> *hanc olim veteres vitam coluere Sabini,*
> *hanc Remus et frater, sic fortis Etruria crevit*
> *scilicet et rerum facta est pulcherrima Roma*
> *septemque una sibi muro circumdedit arces.**[7]

The national theme does not however dominate the *Georgics* to the exclusion of other elements. It is to be noted that when Virgil proclaims his love of the country in Book II he thinks first of Spercheus and Taygetus and the cool valleys of Haemus, not of the Italian countryside;[8] and the conclusion of the fourth book, the story of Aristaeus, with that of Orpheus within it, is thoroughly Greek and indeed Alexandrian in spirit.

In the *Aeneid* the national spirit finds full expression. For more than half the work the scene is laid on Italian soil, and in such episodes as the Trojans' visit to Latinus or that of Aeneas to the site of Rome, and in the catalogues of the Italian and Etruscan chieftains, Virgil gives expression to his love of Italy and of her old traditions. But this is not all. The theme of the *Aeneid* is the foundation of the Roman people; sentiment and antiquarianism are only incidental. Virgil's main purpose is to justify the Roman Empire, and numerous passages look forward to the future and show the greatness of Rome as destined by fate.

> *certe hinc Romanos olim volventibus annis*
> *hinc fore ductores reuocato a sanguine Teucri*

---

* Such was the life the Sabines lived of old,
Such Romulus and Remus; even so
Etruria grew to strength, and Rome surpassed
All other states in glory, with one wall
Girding the union of her seven hills.
                    (L. A. S. JERMYN)

qui mare qui terras omnes dicione tenerent
*pollicitus.**⁹*

So speaks Venus to Jupiter early in the poem, and Jupiter
reassures her; unfolding the secrets of fate, he sets out the future
history of Rome and the boundless empire destined for the
'lords of all, the toga'd race'. When Jupiter learns of Aeneas's
dallying at Carthage he recalls that he is to found a race which
will submit the whole world to the rule of law. In the underworld Anchises foretells the future glories of Aeneas's offspring,
telling how Rome will bound her empire with the world and
her spirit with high heaven, and in Latium Latinus learns from
the oracle of Faunus that the offspring of his future son-in-law
will see the whole world in subjection under their feet.¹⁰

Moreover, Virgil makes it clear that he regards the regime
of Augustus as in accordance with the best traditions of Rome
and as forming the climax of her long history dating back to
Aeneas. In three places he makes specific reference to the
Princeps. In the first book Jupiter foretells the birth of Augustus,
his world-wide conquests and the reign of peace, justice and
order which he is to inaugurate. In the sixth book Anchises
shows to Aeneas a line of Roman heroes culminating in
Augustus, the man who is to restore the Golden Age and extend
the Empire to the furthest east. Finally, on the shield of Aeneas
in Book VIII one of the scenes is the battle of Actium, with
Augustus leading the Italians, standing high on the prow, twin
flames darting from his temples.¹¹

In the sixth book, after he has shown Aeneas the Roman
heroes to be born, Anchises ends his speech with some famous
lines in which Virgil seems to be stating consciously and deliberately what he considers to be Rome's mission in the world:

> *excudent alii spirantia mollius aera,*
> *credo equidem, vivos ducent de marmore vultus,*
> *orabunt causas melius caelique meatus*
> *describent radio et surgentia sidera dicent.*

> *   Surely that from these
> Should one day issue with revolving years
> The Romans, ay, from these the warrior chiefs
> Of Teucer's blood requickened, born to rule
> All potent, sea and land, thou promissedst.
>   (JAMES RHOADES)

tu regere imperio populos, Romane, memento
(hae tibi erunt artes) pacisque imponere morem,
parcere subiectis et debellare superbos.*12

The superiority of others—the Greeks, that is—in sculpture, oratory and astronomy was, with the exception of oratory, beyond dispute, but it was none the less significant that Virgil should resign to them all claims in these fields and limit the arts of the Romans to those of warfare and government. In the time of Cicero the Romans had had the more liberal ambition of equalling the Greeks, if not in the arts and sciences, at least in literature.

Virgil's imperial theme indeed involved some sacrifice of his sensibilities, and his patriotism in the *Aeneid* at times verges on chauvinism. Depreciation of the Greeks in Book II, though no doubt dramatically appropriate, recalls the common Roman self-righteousness in relation to Rome's enemies, and the proud reference in Anchises' speech to the destruction of Corinth contrasts with the regrets Cicero had expressed in *De Officiis*.[13] Virgil has no tears to shed over the fall of the ancient civilization of Greece, to which Rome owed so much. But if the patriotism of the *Aeneid* seems to modern readers to limit the universality of its appeal, it may be doubted whether this would have been felt by, for instance, an educated Greek of Virgil's day. The prevailing philosophy of Stoicism taught that all was predetermined and that mankind was governed by a fate which was the expression of divine reason. If the course of history was a part of this destiny it was hard to resist the conclusion that the Roman Empire was to be accepted as fated and therefore right. The Jupiter of the Stoics, identified with fate and right reason, insensibly merges into Jupiter the guardian god of Rome.

It was not Virgil's purpose in the *Aeneid* to treat of politics

* Some with more grace shall mould the breathing bronze,
Or draw from stone, I trow, the living form,
Plead causes better, map the heavenly paths,
And tell the rising stars. Roman, be thine
To sway the world with Empire. These shall be
Thine arts, to govern with the rule of peace,
To spare the weak and subjugate the proud.
                                        (C. J. BILLSON)

in the narrow sense or to advocate any particular form of government, but certain hints suggest that he had no sympathy with the republican system which had departed. The figure of Drances, the orator and party leader, seems almost a caricature of the republican politician, and if the debate between him and Turnus in Book XI was not deliberately designed to discredit republican politics, at any rate it gives an unfavourable picture of government by discussion, while the simile in Book I of the riot quelled by the *vir pietate gravis ac meritis* suggests that Virgil's preference was for the personal rule of a wise and respected leader.[14] But like Augustus himself, Virgil preferred to emphasise the continuity of the past with the present rather than the break with tradition. It was left for Dante to place Brutus and Cassius in the nethermost hell. Virgil includes the heroes of the Republic in his list of great Romans in Book VI, and when Caesar and Pompey come into the vision he does not take sides. He is content to contrast the harmony of the two while yet unborn with the slaughter they are to cause on earth, and to put into the mouth of Anchises an exhortation against civil war.[15] Cato too finds a place in the *Aeneid*. On the shield of Aeneas one of the pictures is of the punishment of the wicked, with Catiline as the typical sinner, and, in a place apart, the good, with Cato as their lawgiver.[16] Rome did not forget her great men, even when they were on the losing side. It is the same spirit that we find in the great prose writer of the Augustan age, Livy, whom Augustus called a Pompeian and the elder Seneca characterized as *benignus omnibus magnis viris*.[17]

Horace, unlike Virgil, had been a republican, and had fought on the losing side at Philippi. Though in later life he could commemorate the noble death of Cato,[18] his republicanism did not go deep, and he had no difficulty in eventually reconciling himself to a regime which brought happiness and security to himself and to the world in general. In the years following Philippi he seems to have reacted against politics. He was indeed moved by the spectacle of continued civil strife; he exclaims at the criminal folly of his countrymen, turning on each other like wild beasts, and writes of a second generation being wasted by civil war and of Rome bringing on herself the destruction which foreign enemies have been unable to bring about. His remedy however is simply escape, to an imaginary home in the islands of the blest.[19]

But there was another and more practical solution to the ills of the age. In 38 B.C. Horace was introduced to Maecenas and some months later became a member of his circle. The gift of an estate in the Sabine hills cemented the relationship, and by the time the open breach between Antony and Octavian occurred he was firmly on the side of the latter. He shared without reserve in the patriotic emotions aroused by Actium, greeting the death of Cleopatra with joy and relief.[20]

In one of his odes he writes of the ship of state facing new dangers. The occasion is uncertain and the ode enigmatic. But two lines give a clear indication of Horace's change of attitude towards public affairs:

> *nuper sollicitum quae mihi taedium,*
> *nunc desiderium curaque non levis.**[21]

Horace's new concern for the state did not mean an active participation in affairs, like that of his Greek model Alcaeus:

> *tu civitatem quis deceat status*
> *curas et urbi sollicitus times.*†[22]

Affairs of state were Maecenas's business, not Horace's. It was for the poet rather to supply the moral basis of the regime, to preach manly virtue and service to the state, and to celebrate Rome's victories in laudatory odes.

The evils of civil war had impressed themselves deeply on the minds of Horace's generation, and Augustus's regime in its earlier stages was no doubt less secure than it seems to us with our knowledge of subsequent history. Thus reminders of the past and warnings against a renewal of strife were not without relevance even after Actium.

> *audiet cives acuisse ferrum*
> *quo graves Persae melius perirent,*

---

* Not long since a source of concern and weariness to me, now of yearning and anxious care.

† But you for Rome's imperial State
Attend with ever watchful care. (PHILIP FRANCIS)

> *audiet pugnas vitio parentum*
> *rara iuventus.*[*][23]

Rome's external enemies remained, the Britons still unconquered and the Parthians, whose defeat of the Romans at Carrhae remained unavenged. The disgrace of Carrhae suggested to Horace the finest of his 'Roman' odes, that in which he exclaims indignantly against the captive soldiers of Crassus who had married barbarian wives and settled down oblivious of all the ancient traditions of Rome—

> *anciliorum et nominis et togae*
> *oblitus aeternaeque Romae—*[†][24]

and uses with great effect the example of a famous figure of the past, Regulus. But if Rome was to be worthy of her past history she must be able to call on the services of men like those who defeated Pyrrhus and Hannibal, a sturdy peasantry,

> *rusticorum mascula militum*
> *proles Sabellis docta ligonibus*
> *versare glebas.*[‡][25]

The young must learn in the school of warfare, living a hardy life in the open air and experiencing danger; only so will they be feared by Rome's enemies.[26]

But for all his patriotism Horace was less deeply affected by the Augustan spirit than Virgil. His interest in Roman antiquities was slight and his favourite reading was Greek. His *Satires* and *Epistles* show his thought running on the lines of Hellenistic philosophy and little affected by patriotic sentiment, and while his 'Roman' odes cannot be dismissed as insincere, it would be a mistake to overestimate their importance and forget the majority which are free from any obvious national spirit.

---

[*] And yet, less numerous by their Parents' Crimes
  Our sons shall hear, shall hear to latest Times
  Of Roman Arms with civil Gore embru'd,
  Which better had the Persian Foe subdu'd. (PHILIP FRANCIS)
[†] Oblivious of the sacred shields of Mars,
  Oblivious both of toga and of name
  And Vesta's inextinguishable fire. (LORD LYTTON)
[‡] That manly race was born of warriors rustic,
  Tutored to cleave with Sabine spades the furrows.
                    (LORD LYTTON)

The third poet of Maecenas's circle, Propertius, is even less affected by this spirit. Only reluctantly was he drawn out of his private world to a recognition of public affairs. In his first book he is exclusively the poet of love, interested only in himself and Cynthia. The second book shows him now associated with Maecenas, but declining the suggestion that he should write on more serious themes. When in the tenth elegy he consents to sing of war and of Augustus's deeds, he does it self-consciously, seeming to be more interested in himself than in his theme. And one of the poems in this book is in the nature of a defiance of authority and official morality:

> *at magnus Caesar. sed magnus Caesar in armis.*
> *devictae gentes nil in amore valent . . .*
> *unde mihi patriis natos praebere triumphis?*
> *nullus de nostro sanguine miles erit.*[*][27]

In the third book he is still the poet of love, still reluctant to try other themes, still warding off Maecenas's suggestions that he should write on Roman subjects.[28] There is one poem in this book, No. IV, which is inspired by the prospect of an expedition against the Parthians, but it is a strange mixture of the official and the personal. Propertius prophesies in grandiloquent terms the success of the expedition, but he cannot keep frivolity out. He prays for the day when he may witness Caesar's triumph—looking on in the arms of his mistress. Elsewhere in the book he shows something of the Augustan spirit. He attacks Cleopatra with the scorn and bitterness of Horace's ode, but without its generous admiration for the queen's greatness, and he echoes the Virgilian theme of the superiority of Italy to other countries, combining it with the correct imperial and religious sentiment:

> *omnia Romanae cedunt miracula terrae,*
> *natura hic posuit quidquid ubique fuit . . .*
> *nam quantum ferro tantum pietate potentes*
> *stamus: victrices temperat ira manus.*[†][29]

* 'Caesar is mighty.' Yes, but mighty in arms; conquests avail nothing in love. What do I care for producing children to aid the triumphs of Rome? No soldier shall be born of my blood.

† All the marvels of the world yield to the land of Rome; here nature has

Propertius's fourth book at last shows a marked change in his themes. Whether the fire of passion had now burnt itself out or he became genuinely attracted by national subjects, he now yielded to the spirit of the age to the extent of writing in praise of Augustus and in celebration of Actium and composing a number of antiquarian elegies on the legends and traditions of Rome.

Augustus's programme included the reformation of morals, the encouragement of marriage and the family and the limitation of extravagance. An abortive attempt at legislation seems to have been made not long after Actium, but it was not until 18 B.C. that the Julian laws, designed to rehabilitate marriage and stimulate the birth rate, were passed, to be followed in A.D. 9 by the Lex Papia Poppaea. About the same time as the Julian laws various measures were passed to limit extravagance. The way for these measures was prepared by Horace. He laments the decay of marriage and the prevalence of extravagance.[30] With a clear hint of the necessity of official action he writes:

> o quisquis volet impias
>   caedes et rabiem tollere civicam,
> si quaeret pater urbium
>   inscribi statuis, indomitam audeat
> refrenare licentiam.*[31]

This was written before the Julian laws. After they had been passed he can claim with satisfaction:

> nullis polluitur casta domus stupris
> mos et lex maculosum edomuit nefas.†[32]

And in the ode which he placed last in the fourth book and which sums up the achievements of the Augustan age, he writes of the emperor:

---

placed all that is found elsewhere . . . Our strength rests as much on piety as on the sword; even in victory we can restrain our anger.

> * If there be one who hath a care
>   To heal the murderous frenzy of our race,
>   To read upon his statue's base,
>   THE FATHER OF THE CITIES, let him dare
>   To curb the passions of his kind. (EDWARD MARSH)
> † No more adulterers stain our beds,
>   Laws, morals, both that taint efface. (THEODORE MARTIN)

ordinem
rectum evaganti frena licentiae
iniecit emovitque culpas.*[33]

This complacency can hardly have been justified by the facts.
The leaders of thought and taste of the Augustan age did
not set a particularly good example. Virgil and Horace were
bachelors; Propertius was the lover of a *meretrix* and Tibullus
of a married woman; Ovid's *Ars Amatoria* was not written in
celebration of married love. The virtues of a simple peasantry
were easier to praise than to restore—as an Augustan rhetorician put it, 'it is easy to be poor when you have not known
riches'[34]—and it is hard to detect any real change in the moral
tone of Roman society. There was no noticeable abatement
of private extravagance; complaints of the luxury of the age
and the prevailing love of money are common in the literature
of the age, and their continuance in the later years of Augustus's
principate suggests that there was no improvement with time.[35]
It is unlikely that the moralists made much headway against the
general desire for comfort and splendour in private life. In
Tacitus's *Dialogue on Orators* we read of the wealthy and
prosperous householder who requires a house not only sufficient
to keep out rain and wind, but also good to look at, supplied
not only with the necessities of life, but also with gold and
precious stones which he can handle and look at with pleasure.[36]
No doubt there were many such in Rome in all ages. Vitruvius's
complacent remarks on the increasing height of buildings
remind us that the primitivism of poets and preachers was not
shared by practical men; the architects of Rome could hardly
be expected to respond to Horace's praise of the simple nomad
life of the Scythians.[37] Objective evidence concerning social
habits is hard to find, but it may be mentioned that as regards
indulgence in food and drink Tacitus saw no change during
the hundred years from the battle of Actium in 31 B.C. to the
end of the Julio-Claudian dynasty; in his view it was only with
the Flavians that more abstemious habits came in.[38]

In the attacks on luxury and avarice and the praises of

* To righteous order rampant licence curbed,
  Thrust from the state the vices which defile. (LORD LYTTON)

poverty and simplicity so common in the Augustan writers it is often hard to say whether the inspiration comes from national sentiment or from Hellenistic philosophy; but it may be suggested that of the two influences the latter was the stronger. The message of philosophy was superficially the same as that of the old Roman tradition, but there was an important difference. The old Roman had lived an active life of service to the state, whereas the Hellenistic philosophers turned their backs on politics and concentrated on the cultivation of individual self-sufficiency. It may be doubted whether such a philosophy was a very helpful ally to Augustus. For with their constant insistence on simplicity and self-control and their readiness to see greed and self-seeking as the motive of so much of human activity the philosophers went some way towards undermining the belief of the Roman in his own civilization. A strain of pessimism runs through the writings of the Augustan age. It was supposed to be the Golden Age revived, but little satisfaction was to be found in the contemplation of the present. In the rhetorical schools the *locus de saeculo* meant not the celebration of the glories of the age, but an attack on its evils: the declaimer Porcius Latro exclaimed ironically *O nos nimium felici et aureo quod aiunt saeculo natos.**[39] Horace ended one of his odes with the gloomy reflection *aetas parentum peior avis tulit nos nequiores;*† Livy held it to be one of the advantages of history that it enabled him to avert his eyes from the present. Finally, Propertius, for once in prophetic mood, exclaims:

> *frangitur ipsa suis Roma superba bonis.*‡[40]

The age was officially one of martial prowess, but in many the idea of war aroused little enthusiasm. The amatory poets express a frank distaste for war. For them there is no question of duty to the state; if Rome's wars are to be fought it must be by others than themselves.[41] Moreover they see war as prompted simply by greed.[42] Even Horace when addressing

---

* Too happy indeed, too much of a 'Golden Age' is this in which we are born.
† Our fathers' age ignobler than our grandsires
  Bore us yet more depraved. (LORD LYTTON)
‡ Proud Rome is being destroyed by her own prosperity.

Iccius, who was preparing to go to the wars, gives no hint that his friend was performing his duty to the Empire; rather he is credited with coveting the rich treasures of Arabia.[43] We notice too with what disfavour the poets regard commerce and seafaring. While the ordinary man, and the authorities of Rome, might be expected to welcome the recovery of trade which followed the restoration of peace, the intellectuals tended to cling to the idea of primitive self-sufficiency, to condemn the merchant's calling as inspired by greed, and even to make seafaring in itself a symbol of man's audacious ambitions.[44]

Thus in many of the Augustan writers we can observe a curious antithesis between the society in which they lived, and which they accepted and supported, and their moral outlook. In a wealthy and splendid city riches were regarded with feelings of guilt; in an imperial nation with a long martial tradition war was regarded with distaste; in an age which appeared to have every reason for confidence Rome seemed to be destroying herself, unable, as Livy puts it, to bear either her vices or their remedies. Only in Virgil is this antithesis resolved. In the character of Aeneas he provided a model which took account of the moral sensitiveness of the age, but at the same time was not false to Roman tradition. Aeneas was a warrior, but manifestly not one whose sole motive was greed. In him Roman vigour is tamed and purged of its egotism; the man of action becomes the servant of his country and of humanity. Aeneas's task was one of civilization, and this involved hope and confidence in the future. After the fall of Troy he went out to find a new home and found a new people, and this people was to become the Rome of Virgil's own day. The whole conception of the *Aeneid* implied that the task of founding the Roman people was worth while, and Virgil's readers might well feel not only pride in the past but hope for the future. Here at least we seem to find a true Augustan philosophy, an outlook on life that did not turn its back on contemporary society, but accepted it and interpreted it and gave it new meaning.

It has already been suggested that the religious sentiment of the Augustan age was something that belonged essentially to the earlier generation. The same may be said of other aspects of the national spirit. Ovid, for all the antiquarianism of the *Fasti* and his dutiful praises of the imperial house, has little of it. It may well be supposed that the rediscovery of Rome and Italy would lose much of its appeal when the novelty had passed. As Roman society was not easily changed from its luxurious, easy-going ways, so Roman minds continued as before to be more open to influences from Greece and the East than to those of purely Roman origin. Education remained firmly in its Hellenistic mould; the increased prestige of Latin literature meant, it is true, that in the school of the *grammaticus* education was no longer so much weighted in favour of Greek, but the method and character of grammar school teaching remained unchanged, while in the rhetoric school the teaching was even less related to Roman life than it had been under the Republic. Philosophy as before was essentially Greek; the only school of Roman origin, that of Sextius, was shortlived, and in any case hardly distinguishable from Stoicism. The Roman tradition was in fact too weak to satisfy men's minds and spirits, and the Augustan principate, so far from inaugurating a new national culture, ushers in an age when it becomes increasingly difficult to recognize any distinctively Roman contribution to the more or less uniform Greco-Roman culture of the Empire.

THE POLITICAL IDEAS OF THE
EARLY EMPIRE

WITH THE establishment of what was in effect the rule of one
man the older type of political theory which had been be-
queathed from the Greek city states to Republican Rome came
to an end. The relative merits of different types of constitution
was no longer a topic that interested men. To Tacitus oligarchic
or democratic rule was a thing of the past, and the mixed
constitution that Cicero had so much admired was 'easier to
praise than to bring into effect'.[1] No longer was political thought
stimulated by open and free debate, no longer was there that
intimate knowledge of government which men like Cicero
combined with an interest in ideas. Outside the circle of the
emperor's advisers men were condemned to that *inscitia rei
publicae ut alienae* of which Tacitus speaks.[2]

But though the Republic was dead, its memory survived.
Though freedom was lost and could not be recovered, men
were still conscious of its loss. Moreover the character of
Augustus's successors and their advisers made it hard for honest
men to serve both them and their consciences. There remained
at least a personal problem, what attitude one should adopt
towards the ruling power.

The dominating influence in Rome of the early Empire, from
the time of Nero to that of Marcus Aurelius, was Stoicism. The
Stoics had no objection to monarchy in theory. Indeed Seneca
gives it as the Stoic view that the best form of government is
that of a just king, and Stoics of the imperial period are found
elaborating on the virtues of the good king, depicting him as
above the law since he is himself law incarnate, the embodiment
of the divine reason.[3] This was a dangerous doctrine, for, as
Seneca put it, there was no difference between a king and a

tyrant except what lay in his character and behaviour.[4] This meant that if the good king was above the law, the tyrant would be equally so. Law and constitutional forms were irrelevant, and by exalting the good king the philosopher might well make the way easier for the bad. And it was easy to get so into the habit of depicting the king as he should be that the king as he was was ignored, so that the philosopher instructing the monarch becomes scarcely distinguishable from the courtier flattering him. Even Tacitus in the *Dialogus* refers casually to the emperor as 'sapientissimus et unus', which is of course what he ought to have been rather than what he was.[5]

None the less, though the Stoics might be monarchists in theory, in practice individual Stoics might object to particular monarchs. Their philosophy gave them a certain independence. Nothing, they held, could harm the wise man; clinging to the sole good he could afford to lose everything else, could do and say what he thought right in despite of anyone. He might well feel obliged to protest, and opposition to individual acts might develop into, or be represented as, opposition to the whole system. Whether the Stoics of the Empire seriously wished for a restoration of the Republic is doubtful. They looked back to Cato in admiration, but it was an admiration accorded to his character rather than to his politics and was not inconsistent with acceptance of the principate. Tacitus makes one of the characters in his *Dialogue* the author of a work on Cato that caused offence in high quarters; he also makes the same character recognize that there is no going back to the republican past and recommend being content with present circumstances.[6] As Cremutius Cordus argued, it was only right and in accordance with tradition to honour the great Romans of the past.[7]

While Stoicism gave men a moral standpoint from which to criticize the imperial regime, history and literature reminded them that Rome had not always been governed by one man. Higher education was based on a rhetoric that derived from republican days; in the schools the main political theme set for discussion was the reward due to tyrannicide and the prevailing sentiment was a love of liberty. And though the hatred of tyranny expressed in the declamation halls was easily unlearned outside them, there remained the speeches of Cicero, the history of the civil wars and the examples of republican heroes like Cato to feed the mind with a sense of dissatisfaction with the present. Lucan writing under Nero in the sixties of the first century gives poignant expression to the dilemma of a lover of liberty living under a despotism. Thanks to Pharsalus, he says, liberty has retired beyond the Tigris and the Rhine, never to return to Rome; it would have been better if the Romans had never known it and had always lived under a tyranny. The worst fate is to be the subject of a despot and to be ashamed of it; *ex populis qui regna ferunt sors ultima nostra est, quos servire pudet.*[*8]

But though freedom still had some appeal, there were powerful arguments on the other side. In exchange for the loss of freedom Rome had gained security and settled government. The claims of peace were strong, and it could be plausibly represented that the only alternative to the rule of the Caesars was chaos. As one of Lucan's characters puts it, *libertas populi quem regna coercent libertate perit.*[†] Disaster, says Seneca, threatens Rome if the bonds of discipline are broken; she is free in everything except the freedom to perish.[9] To those who looked to Cato or to Brutus and Cassius as their heroes it could be answered that by their time republicanism was already dead and not worth fighting for, and that the civil war was a contest not between freedom and slavery, but between two masters.[10]

Though most Romans were no doubt prepared to admit the claims of *pax* as against *libertas*, Lucan was not such a one. In his later books, at any rate, he makes it clear on which side he stood. The cause of freedom was after all not hopelessly lost. The contest fought out at Pharsalus was, he says, one which will always be with us, the contest between freedom and empire, *libertas* and *Caesar*, and there is a hope that some day Rome will shake off the yoke.[11]

---

* Of all the nations that endure tyranny our lot is the worst; we are ashamed of our slavery.

† When a people is held by tyranny, its freedom is destroyed by freedom.

Seneca, like Lucan, was a Stoic and an admirer of Cato, but unlike him he accepts the Empire and has no sympathy with republicanism. He held the position, flattering to the self-esteem of a philosopher, of tutor and adviser to a young prince, and saw nothing inconsistent with Stoicism in serving the master who he vainly hoped would realize the dreams of philosophers and show himself the good king. Seneca's hope, at any rate in the early years of Nero's rule, was that his pupil would live up to his tutor's exhortations and be a true father to his people. In *De Clementia* he addresses him in flattering terms, and asserts that his subjects are now forced to admit their own happiness.[12]

The question which chiefly exercises Seneca in connection with politics is whether one should engage in public life or not. The Stoics had said that the wise man would play a part in politics, but they had not always practised what they preached.[13] There were Stoics who, contemplating the dangers and ambitions and frustrations of public life, arrived at a position not very different from that of the Epicureans, and recommended withdrawal from politics, comforting themselves with the reflection that the private citizen can do as much good by teaching as the statesman by political activity. Such was the view of one Athenodorus.[14] Seneca censures him as too ready to withdraw from public life, but his own position is not very different. There were times when, affected by the indignities or trivialities of a public career, he was converted to retirement.[15] And he had no difficulty in finding arguments to justify himself. Retirement might sound more Epicurean than Stoic, but it was in accordance with the practice if not the precepts of the founders of Stoicism.[16] Indeed Seneca argues that Stoic precept is also in favour of retirement. Zeno had said that the wise man would engage in politics unless something prevented him, and there were many things which might keep a wise man away from politics.[17] Man is citizen of two states, that into which he is born and the great one comprising gods and men which is the universe. The latter is a commonwealth worthy of a wise man; he remains a member of it in retirement, and can best serve it so. Philosophers like Zeno and Chrysippus have done more for mankind by their teaching than if they had led armies or founded cities.[18]

In later life Seneca's desire for retirement grew stronger. He did not, he was careful to point out, wish merely for ease and idleness; his leisure was devoted to higher things.[19] Public life meant slavery, philosophy true freedom.[20] Retirement was the means to the attainment of *securitas*, freedom from care,[21] and the desire for *securitas* led Seneca a long way from the ideal of Cato. In one of the letters to Lucilius he remarks that it is a mistake to think of philosophers as stubborn, rebellious people, contemptuous of their rulers and governors. On the contrary, no class of persons is more grateful to the ruling power than they, for they owe most to it. The man who leaves the senate house and forum and withdraws to higher pursuits regards with loyalty and affection those who enable him to do this in safety.[22] In another letter, even more remarkable, the philosopher is depicted as a harmless person who gives no offence, and philosophy commended as giving those who pursue it a kind of immunity. We should, says Seneca, avoid giving offence; in any kind of constitution there are those who must be feared, and the wise man will not provoke the anger of the powerful. He will avoid doing so, as one avoids a storm at sea, and will be circumspect even in his philosophy. Seneca is even prepared to suggest that Cato was mistaken in engaging in politics.[23]

In all this we can perhaps detect signs of an uneasy conscience. Seneca had after all played some part in public affairs, but it had been an unheroic part. He had compromised for too long, and could only hope for escape. It was left to others to show that the spirit of Cato was not dead, and that Stoics were not always content to accept the imperial power with gratitude and retire to a harmless seclusion. It is in the reign of Nero that the 'philosophical opposition' familiar to historians of the period first comes to the fore. Though it often went with admiration for republican heroes like Brutus and Cato, it was not, so far as one can see, based on any theory of government or directed against monarchy as such. It was, rather, inspired by the austere morality of Stoicism and directed against a

vicious and decadent court. Men like Thrasea and Barea Soranus
were prepared to resist and criticize acts which they thought
wrong, or to show their disapproval as Thrasea did by deliberate
abstention from the senate. The emperor's servile supporters
interpreted such independence as disloyalty, playing on the unpopularity of the austere moralist, hinting that disapproval
meant revolutionary designs, claiming that Stoicism made men
disturbers of the peace and supporters of a liberty that meant
the destruction of the Empire.[24]

The condemnation of Thrasea gave Stoicism a martyr whose
death recalled that of Cato. His example inspired his son-in-law,
Helvidius Priscus, who was, like him, a Stoic and had derived
from him, according to Tacitus, above all else the spirit of
liberty.[25] Helvidius's opposition to Vespasian cost him his life.
His conduct is represented by Dio as that of a violent revolutionary, an enemy of monarchy who cultivated the favour of
the mob, and an unworthy follower of Thrasea.[26] Such, however, was not the view of Tacitus. There were, he says, some
who thought him too greedy for fame, but his own considered
judgment represents him as an upright and admirable character,
and gives no support to Dio's picture, which is indeed so inconsistent with the character of a Stoic and Roman senator as
to be in itself highly improbable.[27]

Teachers of philosophy shared in the suspicions of disloyalty
which their pupils aroused, and there were expulsions of them
under Vespasian in A.D. 71, and Domitian in 89 and 95. Whereas
in the case of men like Thrasea and Helvidius we can only infer
their political doctrines, we have more evidence in the case of
the professed philosophers, where either writings or a record of
their teaching survives. The philosophers appear to have been
either monarchists, like Dio of Prusa, who rejects democracy
as quite impracticable,[28] or essentially unpolitical, like Epictetus.
Epictetus, who was among those banished by Domitian in 89,
does not regard it as his business to alter the arrangements of
this life, but rather to do what the statesman cannot do, give
peace and tranquillity of mind. 'See', he says, 'Caesar provides
us with profound peace; there are no wars any longer, no battles,
no large scale brigandage or piracy; at any hour we may travel

by land or sail from the rising to the setting of the sun. But can he give us peace from fever or shipwreck, fire, earthquake, lightning? Can he give us peace from love, sorrow, envy? No, from none of these things. It is for philosophical teaching to give men peace from these.'[29] The political problem seemed solved with the establishment of peace and security. There remained the moral problem, the cultivation of a mind at peace, free from all disturbances and independent of circumstances. This is the only freedom that matters to Epictetus. The word freedom is often on his lips, but it has nothing to do with politics or outward circumstances, and it is compatible with imprisonment and slavery. Chains and torture are irrelevant; they only affect the body, not the real self. 'The free man is the man who lives as he wills, who is subject to neither compulsion nor hindrance nor force, whose choices are unhampered, whose desires attain their end.'[30] It is not wealth, honours and kingdoms that make a man free; it is the knowledge of the right way of living, the recognition that the only thing that matters is what cannot come under compulsion from outside, the προαίρεσις or moral purpose. 'That man is free to whom all things happen according to his moral purpose.'[31]

A Stoic of the type of Epictetus would submit to anything except where his προαίρεσις was involved. He would not do what he thought wrong. And here the inner freedom of the philosopher might become in a sense political. 'The tyrant' or 'Caesar' in Epictetus is a hostile power who may put the good man in prison or take his life. But the good man's resistance would be passive. Epictetus's teaching might produce martyrs, but would hardly produce revolutionaries.

Stoicism, powerful though its influence was, must always have been confined to a comparatively small circle. The ordinary educated Roman no doubt regarded the philosophers, as the younger Pliny did, with a respectful detachment, while some, like Quintilian, were actively hostile. When Agricola's mother dissuaded him from pursuing philosophy beyond what befitted a Roman and a senator, she rightly sensed that the devoted life the Stoics demanded could hardly be reconciled with a public career.[32] The Roman who followed such a career would be content to do his duty as best he could. The business of government and administration must be carried on, and it could not be carried on by unpractical idealism and heroic gestures of defiance. Philosophy may have made an appeal in youth, but *mox mitigavit ratio et aetas.*[33]

Such a one, perhaps, was Tacitus. He was not a philosopher, but neither would he, like Quintilian, dismiss philosophers with impatient sneers. He felt deeply the difficulty of combining high ideals with loyal service to the state; he had lived through the reign of Domitian, had seen good men put to death and had himself acquiesced. He admired the martyrs of Stoicism, Thrasea and Barea Soranus, 'virtue incarnate' as he calls them, and Helvidius Priscus, of whom he writes in terms of such high praise.[34] But he believed that it was better, or at least as good, to go on doing one's job quietly and conscientiously even under a bad emperor. He records of Agricola that 'he did not court fame and death by obstinacy and a futile parade of independence', and goes on to say: 'Those whose way it is to admire what is forbidden should realize that great men can exist even under bad emperors, and that obedience and moderation if united with industry and energy can reach the same height of fame to which many have climbed by the steep path, gaining glory by a spectacular death without any advantage to the state.'[35] So in his latest work he suggests that it is possible to steer a middle course free from ambition and danger, between grovelling subservience and dangerous defiance.[36]

Tacitus was a complex character, and it would be misleading to label him either conformist or republican. The *Dialogue on Orators,* if it is his earliest work, shows how even before he began writing history he had meditated on the great change that took place in the affairs of Rome with the transition from Republic to Principate. In the speech of Maternus which ends the dialogue we have what is no doubt Tacitus's own contribution to the question he is discussing, the decline of oratory. His thesis is that oratory depends on the state of society, and that the oratorical glories of the Ciceronian age necessarily perished with the Republic that gave them birth. But the development of this theme is not that of an admirer of republican liberty.

'Great and distinguished oratory is the nursling of licence which fools call liberty, the associate of sedition, the goad of a lawless populace, undisciplined, irresponsible, overbearing, thoughtless, arrogant, something which does not grow in well ordered states.'[37] Peace is better than war, but war breeds more good soldiers; so it is with oratory. Oratory, like everything else, had been pacified by Augustus.[38] Let us then, Maternus concludes, be content with our own times. 'Since no one can at the same time achieve great glory and great peace, let each man enjoy the blessings of his own age without disparaging another age.'[39]

After Tacitus's experience of Domitian's tyranny he viewed the Empire in a less favourable light. 'Sapientissimus et unus', the phrase used of the emperor in the *Dialogue*, is not paralleled in the other works. The blessings of peace seemed less attractive, the loss of opportunities for greatness more to be regretted. With the establishment of peace 'there was an end of great men'—*magna illa ingenia cessere*. Character deteriorated under despotism, servility and adulation became the rule. Truth was undermined, at first from an ignorance of public affairs, afterwards by the spirit of adulation on the one hand and hatred towards the ruling power on the other.[40] The historian of the Republic could tell of great battles and political conflicts; Tacitus's theme by contrast is narrow and inglorious, a dull and gloomy story, only justified by its instructiveness, since those who live under the rule of one man must know the ways of despots.[41]

And yet in spite of regrets for the past, the Empire must be accepted. 'The interests of peace required the rule of one man.' Augustus 'won over everyone by the charms of peace. . . . All preferred the safety of the present to the dangers of the past.'[42] In the debate between *pax* and *libertas,* empire and republic, we cannot say that Tacitus definitely took one side or the other. Perhaps it would be true to say that his heart was on the side of the republican past, his head on the side of the imperial present.

Much the same might be said of Tacitus's attitude toward another aspect of politics, Roman imperialism. His sympathies went out to the peoples whose freedom Rome had taken away, but intellectual conviction made him a supporter of the imperial power. He pays a generous tribute to Rome's enemy Arminius, 'without doubt the liberator of Germany', and puts into the mouth of the British chieftain Calgacus that condemnation of Roman imperialism which is summed up in the memorable sentence 'solitudinem faciunt, pacem appellant'.[43] The healthy, courageous life of the tribes described in the *Germania* contrasts with the luxurious sophistication of Rome. Even the wise and enlightened policy of Romanization carried out by the admired Agricola is described by Tacitus with a sneer. The Britons took to Roman dress and the toga, and 'little by little they descended to alluring vices, colonnades and baths and elegant dinners. This was called culture by the ignorant Britons, though really it was a feature of slavery.'[44]

Freedom, Lucan had said, had retired beyond the Tigris and the Rhine. Tacitus could not withhold sympathy from those who still retained or had recently lost this freedom. Yet he would presumably have subscribed to the reasoned defence of the Roman Empire which he put into the mouth of Cerealis in the *Histories*. Addressing the rebellious Gauls, Cerealis argues that until she acknowledged Roman power Gaul was the victim of warring chieftains. After her victory Rome imposed no burdens on the defeated apart from what was necessary for the preservation of peace. Peace was impossible without armies, and armies meant taxation. Apart from this there was no discrimination against the Gauls; it was open to them to command armies and rule provinces. There were injustices in Roman rule, but these must be endured like bad harvests. There would be wrongdoing as long as mankind lasted, but it was not continuous and was balanced by better things. If the Roman power were to be destroyed, there would be nothing but war between one tribe and another. Eight hundred years of tradition had constructed a fabric which could not be destroyed without the ruin of those who destroyed it. 'So, then, love and cherish peace and that Rome in which conquerors and conquered enjoy equal rights; be taught by the examples of either fortune not to prefer resistance with destruction to obedience with security.'[45]

Peace or liberty. The same dilemma faced the provincials as the senators of Rome. On the whole the subject peoples accepted the Roman peace as the senators did the peace of the principate, and for the latter at any rate the dilemma seemed solved and the debate closed when Nerva, in Tacitus's words, 'united the two previously incompatible things, the principate and liberty'.[46] The tensions set up by Julio-Claudian and Flavian despotism were resolved, the memory of the Republic grew dimmer and opposition became a thing of the past. The philosophers returned to favour. Trajan listened to lectures on kingship from Dio of Prusa, and in the person of Marcus Aurelius the successor of Domitian was united with the spiritual successor of Epictetus.

It is to the Stoics of the opposition that Marcus Aurelius looks back as his masters in political theory. He records that from his brother Severus he had learned to know 'Thrasea, Helvidius, Cato, Dion, Brutus, and to conceive the idea of a state of equal laws, governed in accordance with equality and free speech and of a kingship that honours most the freedom of the governed'.[47] The words which he uses, πολιτεία ἰσόνομος, ἰσηγορία, belong essentially to the city-state democracy of fifth-century Athens, and seem of little relevance to the vast centralized empire of the Antonine age. Political liberty could hardly flourish after so many years of despotism and the indifference to public affairs which it bred. And philosophy fostered the same spirit. Stoicism had become primarily a way of cultivating the inner self, and for those who followed this way what mattered most was their own moral state. Marcus Aurelius himself shows little interest in the political task. His heart was not in his work. Life at court was for him like a stepmother, to whom one is obliged by duty to pay one's respects; his true mother was philosophy. 'Go to her often and refresh yourself with her, and she will make the court seem tolerable to you and you tolerable in it.'[48] It was not the society in which he lived and which he ruled to which he gave his allegiance, but rather the great society of the universe which included all rational beings. 'I am by nature a reasonable and social creature; my city and fatherland as Antoninus is Rome, as a human being is the universe.' 'The poet says "Dear city of Cecrops;" wilt thou not rather say, "Dear city of Zeus"?'[49]

Unam omnium rempublicam agnoscimus mundum.[50] The words of Tertullian might have been used by the Stoic emperor. The way was prepared for the Christians, strangers and sojourners on earth, their citizenship not of this world.

X

FATE AND THE GODS

THERE IS perhaps no passage in Tacitus more surprising to a modern reader than that in which, after remarking on the wisdom and political success of Lepidus under Tiberius, he adds the words: 'and this forces me to wonder whether the favour of the emperors towards some and their dislike of others is, like all else, a matter of fate and the chances of birth, or whether something rests with our own designs'.[1] Tacitus's doubts about the possibility of man shaping his own career are strange in a historian, whose subject, the actions of men in society, seems almost to presuppose freewill. They are, however, in keeping with the fatalism current in his day. The world appeared to be governed either by blind chance or by a fixed destiny; the choice lay between these two explanations. 'I find it hard to decide', writes Tacitus elsewhere, 'whether human affairs are governed by fate and immutable destiny or by chance.' Lucan offers the same alternative to his readers, and the elder Pliny, reviewing contemporary religious opinions, tells us that all over the world men worship Fortuna, which in this context is to be equated with chance, while 'others attribute events to their star and the laws of birth, holding that god has laid down the future for all time and intervened no further'.[2]

Among the believers in destiny must be reckoned the Stoics, though they placed their own interpretation on the idea, and were not to be classed with the ordinary fatalists, the consulters of astrologers and soothsayers. As Tacitus puts it, they held that affairs did not depend on the wandering stars, but were determined by the beginnings and sequences of natural causation.[3] Moreover Stoic orthodoxy identified fate with God and reason and nature, so that fate meant something more than what was inevitably determined and to accept fate was to be in harmony with the divine reason. The traditional Stoic doctrine is reasserted by Seneca. 'We understand Jove as ruler and guardian of the universe, soul and spirit of the world, lord and author of creation, to whom all names are fitting. If you wish to call him fate, you will not be wrong; it is he from whom all things depend, the cause of causes. If you wish to call him providence, you will be right; it is he whose wisdom takes counsel for this world. . . . If you wish to call him nature, you will not be mistaken; it is he from whom all things are born, by whose breath we live. If you wish to call him the universe, you will not err; he is himself all that you see, immanent in all its parts, maintaining himself and all that is his.'[4] Similarly in another work, after praising the gifts of our maker, Seneca goes on to answer the objection that these are the gifts of nature. 'What else is nature but God and the divine reason immanent in the universe and its parts?' And he adds that God may also be called fate, as being the original cause from which the whole nexus of cause and effect depends.[5]

Since the Stoic god, identified with fate, was also the beneficent providence which takes counsel for the world, it was right that man should be duly grateful to him. It is easy, says Epictetus, to find occasion to praise providence, if one takes a comprehensive view. All nature reveals the divine artificer. Animals are created for man's use.[6] Man is foolish to complain because the beasts have everything provided for them by nature; this is part of the divine scheme, for as they were designed for our service, it is only right that they should be ready for use and in no need of further attention. Man, then, should be constantly hymning and praising the deity for his benefits. 'As we dig and plough and eat we should sing to god: "Great is god that he has provided us with these instruments by which we till the earth; great is god that he has given us hands, the power to swallow, the belly, the gift of growing unconsciously and breathing while asleep." This we should sing on all occasions, and the greatest and most divine of our hymns should be in thanks for the gift of comprehending all this and following in the way.'[7]

This belief in a beneficent providence was not without its difficulties. In the time of Lucretius men had pointed to those features in nature which seemed to contradict it. Now it was rather the difficulties of the individual which hindered assent to the doctrine. Apart from the ordinary annoyances and discomforts of life which made some complain against providence,[8] there was the problem presented by the spectacle of the good man suffering. If the gods cared for man, as Ennius put it, *bene bonis sit, male malis, quod nunc abest.*[9] The correct Stoic answer was that the ills which afflicted the good were not ills at all. As Tacitus put it: 'Good and ill are not what the common people suppose them to be; many who appear to battle against adversity are blessed, many amid great wealth are utterly miserable, if the former bear their hard lot firmly and the latter make foolish use of their prosperity.'[10] This view, however, was not easy to accept, for it might well be supposed that if the physical world was so ordered as to serve the needs of mankind, human society likewise would in some degree reflect the divine providence. It should be remembered that the Stoics had no belief in a judgment hereafter that might reverse the judgment of this world.

Thus there was a real difficulty for the Stoic, and Lucan, Stoic though he was, was moved to deny all providential governance of the world. In a passage of impassioned declamation, speaking in his own person, he exclaims:

> sunt nobis nulla profecto
> numina: cum caeco rapiantur saecula cursu,
> mentimur regnare Iovem.*[11]

The subject matter of Lucan's poem made the problem perhaps more acute for him than it was for Stoics who were concerned only with philosophical theory or personal morality. Should the process of history be accepted as the expression of a benevolent destiny? If so, the extinction of liberty and all that followed must be part of the designs of providence. But *victrix causa deis placuit sed victa Catoni.* Fate was not on the side of Cato, and Lucan chooses the losing side. In the days of Augustus it

---

* There are no gods; to say Jove reigns is wrong;
'Tis a blind chance that moves the years along.

had been possible for Virgil, surveying the whole course of Roman history, to see in it the fulfilment of destiny; but the optimism of Virgil's day had passed away, and now Fate seemed more maleficent than beneficent. The words 'Fate' and 'the gods' are used by Lucan in the sense not of a beneficent providence guiding the course of history, but of a historical process which frustrates and defeats the better cause.[12]

Others besides Lucan felt the difficulties of Stoic orthodoxy. In his *De Providentia* Seneca set out to meet the difficulty of reconciling the ills suffered by the good with the idea of providence. His main argument is that sufferings are a discipline; God is like a stern father who educates his offspring in a hard school. Virtue needs an adversary; there is no finer sight for the gods than that of Cato standing erect amid the ruins of the state and finding his way to freedom through death. Human greatness is not discovered until it is tested; we must be hardened against fortune by fortune itself.[13] Seneca argues further that the ills which afflict the good are not really ills; they benefit not only the sufferer but mankind in general. They show how mistaken are the commonly accepted values; if the good man were rewarded by the goods of this world, this would be taken as proof that they were real goods. Finally the good man accepts his fate willingly, and 'it is a great consolation to be carried along with the universe'.[14] Adversity, Seneca argues elsewhere, should be accepted as part of destiny. Nothing is miserable to the good man, because all things are in accordance with nature. In adversity he gives to god not his obedience but his assent; he follows not because he must, but because he wishes to. Seneca quotes the lines in which Cleanthes had written of a joyful submission to destiny, adding his own epigrammatic summary, which expresses as well as can be expressed in a few words the Stoic idea of Fate: 'Fate leads the willing follower, but drags the unwilling.'[15]

A century or so later, later than Seneca Fronto, after a number of losses in his family circle, was bereft of his grandson. In the letter which he wrote to Marcus Aurelius on this occasion, a letter which remains moving in spite of occasional pedantries, he complains of the injustice of providence, which makes no distinction between the good and the bad, and has robbed a blameless man of a loved son. He comforts himself, however, with the thought that death may be really not an evil but a blessing, removing us from the fetters of the body to a tranquil and blessed existence. 'This,' he adds, 'I would more readily believe than that all human affairs are guided either by no providence or by an unjust one.'[16]

Fronto was no philosopher. He represents the piety of the average educated man, who continued to cherish, though with no great confidence, the idea of a life of bliss hereafter as at any rate a possible alternative to annihilation. 'If', writes Tacitus at the end of the *Agricola*, 'there is some abode for the shades of the good, if, as philosophers hold, the souls of the great are not extinguished with the body. . . .'[17] Survival was a wistful hope, based on no firm conviction; it found no real support in the theories of the dominant philosophy, for the Stoic view was that after death the soul merges with the world soul of which it is a part, and such a form of survival was hardly to be distinguished from annihilation.

The Stoics often speak of God and the gods, but they can hardly be said to have a true religious feeling. The humility and reverence of religion is alien to Stoicism. It is possible to quote sentences from Seneca, as Lactantius did, which the Christian can readily appropriate,[18] but, as Coleridge said, 'you may get a motto for every sect or line of thought in Seneca'. Holding that the divine was to be found in the human soul no less than in the universe, Seneca prefers to dwell on the greatness of man rather than on that of God. Jupiter, he says, quoting Sextius, has no more power than the good man. He may have more that he can give to others, but of two good men the richer is not the better; Jupiter only excels the good man in being good for longer, and the latter does not value himself any the less because his virtues are confined into a narrower space of time. Indeed the wise man might be said to have the advantage over Jupiter in that while both look on the possessions of others with indifference, the former is unwilling to make use of them while the latter is unable to.[19] Thus the wise man may well be accorded that reverence which the ordinary man gives to groves and other sacred places. If you see a man unterrified by dangers, untouched by desires, happy in adversity, calm in the midst of storms, looking on man from above and gods from a level, does not, asks Seneca, a sense of reverence come over you?[20] In the same spirit Lucan finds in Cato a worthy object of worship. 'Lo, a true father of his country, most worthy of Rome's altars, one by whom none will be ashamed to swear, and whom, if ever she stands free from servitude, she will, some day, make a god.'[21] Epictetus, with his exultant praise of the deity and his reverent references to 'another' who provides for mankind and watches over him, is more religious in tone and less arrogant in his claims for man. But he too regards the true philosopher as one who 'desires to become god instead of man', and bids man have 'no ignoble or humble thoughts of himself'.[22]

The traditional practices of ancient religion were regarded with scant sympathy by the Stoics. In his lost *De Superstitione* Seneca attacked various contemporary cults in terms which St Augustine was glad to borrow.[23] Prayers, sacrifices and acts of worship were unnecessary. What need of prayers? he asks. Make yourself happy, *fac te ipsum felicem*.[24] He allows, it is true, that prayer may be of some use if what is prayed for is in accordance with fate.[25] But a more common theme is that God's nature is itself good and the best form of worship is to imitate his goodness.[26] Marcus Aurelius recommends prayer not for the blessings of life but for the ability to do without them. If the gods can co-operate with man, they can co-operate for this end. Prayer cannot alter events, but it may produce the right state of mind in relation to events.[27]

Turning from the philosophers to the satirists we find Persius, while not rejecting the practice of prayer, condemning unworthy and selfish petitions and concluding that the right offering to the gods is a pure heart, while Juvenal develops the theme into a satire on the vanity of all human prayers. Leave to the gods, he concludes, to decide what is in our best interest. If you must pray, pray for health of mind and body, for strength and self-control. But, he adds, these qualities are what man can provide himself. Virtue for Juvenal, as for the professed Stoics, is essentially something to be attained by man's own efforts.[28]

Thus religion in the early Empire found little support in philosophy. Whereas later Platonism succeeded in uniting philosophy with traditional religion, no such union was effected by the Stoics of the Empire. They had none of Virgil's reverent feeling for established religious practice. The antiquarianism and patriotic sentiment that was so closely bound up with Roman religious feeling meant little to them, for the Stoic creed taught men to be citizens of the world free from the ties of any local or national sentiment. Neither the Spaniard Seneca nor the Phrygian Epictetus would have any natural inherited sympathy with Roman religion, and the philosophy which they shared would not require it of them or impart it to them.

The state religion, revived and re-established by Augustus, continued to be practised under his successors, but though Jupiter Capitolinus might grace the perorations of speeches on public occasions,[29] men's private thoughts did not dwell on his power or his beneficence. The burning of the Capitoline temple might arouse Tacitus's indignation, and the solemn ceremonies of its rebuilding his sympathetic interest,[30] but his historical writing shows no faith in the power of Jupiter as guardian deity of Rome. When he writes of the gods it is of their wrath rather than of their favour.

With the end of the Flavian dynasty in A.D. 96 it became easier to believe that a divine power guided the affairs of Rome. It was no mere chance, according to Pliny, that gave Trajan to Rome as emperor. It was rather the work of the gods; he was chosen 'not by the secret power of the fates but by Jove himself, openly and in the presence of all'.[31] Prosperity and settled government favoured the established religion, and in the second century there was even something of a revival of religious sentiment. The antiquarianism of the Antonine age provided a favourable climate for a traditional piety. Religious formulae are common in the letters of Fronto. 'I pray to the gods', he writes, 'every morning for Faustina.' He pays his vows before the Lares and Penates and household gods, and while in the country prays for Verus's health 'at all the hearths, altars, sacred groves and consecrated trees'.[32] Marcus Aurelius himself as Emperor of Rome had a special interest in the state religion, and was a scrupulous performer of its rites. When appointed to the college of the Salii in his eighth year he carried out the rites conscientiously, learning all the formulae by heart, and in later life he was no less scrupulous.[33] Yet what has been said above of his Stoic predecessors applies no less to him; he did not effect a union of philosophy and traditional religion. In his *Meditations* he writes of God and the gods and of the divine providence, and includes 'reverence for the gods' among the duties of man,[34] but he remains an orthodox Stoic whose god is reason, the universal spirit in man and in nature. He has less sense of a personal god than Epictetus, and less than any man perhaps would he feel the need for the support of ritual or myth in his personal religion. 'That man lives with the gods indeed who all life long opens his soul to them well content with the dispensations of providence and executing every wish of that deity, that portion of himself, which Zeus has given man to be his guardian and his guide. And this deity is each man's mind and reason.'[35] It is the god within that is man's guide, and it is enough for him to do it service.[36] And the Zeus that has implanted in each man a part of himself is universal nature, that impersonal power to which Marcus Aurelius submits himself. 'Whatever is agreeable to thee, O universe, is agreeable also to me. Nothing is too early or too late for me that is in time for thee. All is fruit for me which thy seasons bear, O nature. Out of thee are all things and in thee and unto thee.'[37] This austere, impersonal faith has little connection with the cults of Rome. In Marcus Aurelius the relation of religion to philosophy was much as it had been in the days of Cicero. Religion appealed to sentiment, philosophy to the intellect; religion belonged to the public personality, philosophy to the private.

The main strength of Roman religion lay, as in earlier days, in its association with patriotic sentiment. The gods, it was felt, had given Rome her world-wide Empire, and her safety and prosperity depended on the continuance of the old worship. This theme, which we met in the speeches of Cicero, reappears in the last days of paganism in the appeal of Symmachus on behalf of the Altar of Victory, and in the arguments of those pagans whom Augustine confuted in the *City of God*. Its appeal was one to which many would respond, but it could not stand up against rational argument or spiritual conviction, and Roman religion suffered the fate which probably awaits any religion, however long-lived and venerated it may be, which is nothing more than the expression of national sentiment. The pagan spokesman in the *Octavius* of Minucius Felix bases his argument for his religion on tradition and patriotism; let us worship, he says in effect, as our ancestors worshipped and main ain the religion which made Rome great.[38] His case is weak, and no doubt the author intended that it should be, but it is hard to see what better argument for Roman religion he could have produced.

XI

THE STOIC WAY OF LIFE

In the period from Nero to Marcus Aurelius Stoicism was beyond question the dominant philosophy at Rome. Controversy aroused only a languid interest and dissentient voices were hardly heard. There was virtually only one way to wisdom, the Stoic way. Even within the school there was little interest in the niceties of doctrine; Stoicism was less a system of thought than a way of life. It was embraced not so much because of intellectual conviction as because it provided the means to a good life. 'No longer', writes Marcus Aurelius, 'engage in general discussion about the nature of the good man, but be a good man.'[1]

Whatever may have been the official doctrine of the school about determinism and freewill, the whole of the teaching of later Stoicism was based on the possibility of choice. The word προαίρεσις, choice or moral purpose, is constantly on the lips of Epictetus. Seneca recognizes the importance of the will. 'What do you need', he asks, 'to be a good man?' and answers, 'The will to be'. And this will to be good is something that cannot be learned: *velle non discitur*.[2] The Stoicism of Seneca marks a break with the intellectualism of earlier Greek thought; it was no longer assumed that to know what was right meant to do what was right. The wise man and the good man were still identified, but there was a shift of emphasis from wisdom to goodness, from knowledge to the will.

Thus we find among the Stoics of the Empire a new emphasis on the personality of the teacher as opposed to the teaching. The history of Stoicism in this period is the history not of a development of doctrine, but of a series of teachers who inspired admiration and discipleship by their example and their personality as well as by their arguments and their eloquence.

Seneca has recorded the impression made on him as a young man by the Stoic Attalus. He was the first to arrive and the last to leave the class; when he heard Attalus declaim against the vices and miseries of life he was moved to pity the human race; when Attalus praised poverty, he felt a desire to be poor; when he attacked pleasures, he resolved to practise self-denial. Another impressive preacher was Sotion the Pythagorean, under whose influence Seneca took up vegetarianism for a time.[3] More intimate was the relationship of Persius to his master Cornutus. The poet describes how at adolescence he put himself in the charge of this second Socrates, and how the philosopher's rule straightened the twists of his character and moulded his spirit by reason:

> tecum etiam longos memini consumere soles
> et tecum primas epulis decerpere noctes:
> unum opus et requiem pariter disponimus ambo
> atque verecunda laxamus seria mensa.*[4]

The spirit of discipleship is found too in the last of the Roman Stoics, Marcus Aurelius, who 'so honoured his teachers that he kept golden statues of them in his household shrine and ever honoured their tombs with visits, victims and flowers',[5] and has left in his *Meditations* a moving record of what he owed to others.

Man, it is recognized, needs help. 'No one', writes Seneca, 'by himself has sufficient strength to rise; he must have someone to stretch out a hand and help him out.' And it is not the eloquent preachers who help most, but 'those who teach by their lives, who show by their actions that right course of which they have spoken, who teach what is to be avoided and are never discovered doing it. Choose a helper whom you can admire more when you see him than when you hear him.'[6] Such a one

* Can I forget, how many a summer's day,
  Spent in your converse, stole, unmark'd away?
  Or how, while listening with increas'd delight,
  I snatch'd from feasts, the earlier hours of night?
  —One time (for to your bosom still I grew)
  One time of study, and of rest, we knew;
  One frugal board where, every care resign'd,
  An hour of blameless mirth relax'd the mind. (GIFFORD)

was Epictetus, who practised the ascetic, disciplined life that
he preached, who wrote nothing, but attracted devoted followers
and readily gave help and advice to those who brought him
their problems and difficulties. The helping hand might come
not only from the living but from the dead also. 'When you
have progressed', writes Seneca to Lucilius, 'enough to respect
yourself, you may dismiss your attendant (*paedagogus*). Mean-
while protect yourself by some great man from the past, Cato
or Scipio or Laelius, someone whose appearance would cause
even the worst of men to hide their faults.'[7]

The teacher helps the pupil by advice as well as by example.
Seneca collects texts and sends quotations to Lucilius in the
hope that he will find them useful. He recommends self-
examination at the end of the day, a practice which Sextius
had taken over from the Pythagoreans and which Seneca
himself followed.[8] He gives various practical suggestions for
the conquest of anger, recommends exercise and games for
some, and advises others to read poetry or other soothing
literature.[9] Similarly Epictetus suggests counting the days on
which one has not been angry as a help towards weakening the
habit.[10]

Zeno's message that man should live in accordance with
nature and that virtue is the sole good remains fundamental
for the later Stoics. There is, however, nothing narrow and
exclusive about their doctrine; Seneca in particular is prepared
to criticize the founder of Stoicism,[11] and to borrow examples
and precepts from other schools, Pythagorean, Cynic, even
Epicurean. Certain features of early Stoicism have faded into
the background. The idea of the great gulf between virtue and
vice has given place to that of a gradual progress towards
perfection; and though Seneca defends the paradoxes, he does
so without much conviction, and one gets the impression that
this was a part of Zeno's message that had outlived its usefulness.[12] On the other hand, the later Stoics look back to the
founders of the school rather than to men like Panaetius and
Posidonius. Zeno and Chrysippus provide the authentic doctrine,
even if orthodoxy at times sits lightly on their later followers.

Thus the ideal set up for mankind was still represented in

the figure of the wise man, invulnerable to injury and ill fortune, consistent and self-sufficient, subject to neither hopes nor fears, conscious of his own superiority and so impervious to insult.[13] The emotions must be subdued. The wise man will not be angry, even if he sees his father killed and his mother raped.[14] He will be free from the weakness of pity, which Seneca compares to laughing when others laugh and yawning when they yawn.[15] The flesh must be disciplined. Luxuries are unnecessary and enervating; only a little is needed for food and clothing, and the man who accustoms himself to living within the bounds of nature will have no cause to fear poverty.[16]

There was of course nothing new about such teaching. But it had lost nothing of its force with the passage of time. Under the early Empire, in spite of the peace and security which, generally speaking, was established throughout the Roman world, life was far from secure for those who played some part in public life, and a philosophy which trained men to bear the blows of fortune was of real relevance. But it may also be suggested that Stoicism owed something of its appeal not to the hardness but to the easiness of the times. The wealthier Romans of the early Empire lived an easy life so far as material circumstances were concerned; with armies of slaves to manage their property and minister to their comfort they were free to spend their time as they wished, in self-indulgence, recreation, gossiping, travel, dilettantism.[17] Sometimes this life of ease proved profoundly boring, and among the diseases of the age was that *taedium vitae* which Seneca analyses so powerfully. He distinguishes various types of tedium, but all of them are characterized by dissatisfaction with self, by restlessness and inability to use leisure. 'We are so weak that there is nothing we can bear; we cannot endure work or pleasure, we cannot endure ourselves or anything for long. This has led some to death, because by constantly changing their purpose they kept returning to the same point and left no room for novelty. They begin to be bored with life and the world and there comes to them the question of the pleasure seeker whose luxuries have lost their savour: "How long the same round?" (*Quousque eadem*?)'[18] If there is anything in Seneca's analysis of the malaise of his times, it may well be that the heroic self-discipline of Stoicism appealed to some as providing a way out of the tedium of aimless pleasure seeking.

Certainly the philosophers, whether they were Stoics or their near allies the Cynics, emphasized that theirs was no easy way, and even welcomed adversity as a means to test themselves. Demetrius the Cynic said that nothing could be worse than the lot of the man who never suffered adversity, and called a life unaffected by the blows of fortune a dead sea. Seneca, who quotes this remark with approval, adds the comment that to live in undisturbed ease is not tranquillity but a dead calm, and elsewhere, describing his feelings on reading an inspiring work by Sextius, he compares himself to Ascanius in the *Aeneid* looking for a foaming boar or a lion to test himself and show his manliness. I want, adds Seneca, something to conquer.[19]

Passages like this suggest that a too easy life might produce by way of reaction a desire for something sterner and harder. There were in Seneca's day some who amused themselves with imitating the life of the poor out of boredom with wealth, playing with the simple life as a change from luxury.[20] Seneca, who has been advising Lucilius to practise fasting, is careful to point out that he does not mean this sort of trifling, but it is not altogether easy to draw a line between the self-mortification of the dilettante in search of new experiences and the discipline of the true Stoic. There is an interesting letter of Seneca describing how a friend of his, suffering from an incurable disease, was considering whether to put an end to his life. Another friend, a Stoic, gave him the following advice: 'Do not worry as if it was a great matter you are considering. Living is no great thing; all your slaves live, all animals live. It is a great thing to die honourably, wisely, bravely. Think how often you repeat the same action—food, sleep, sexual desire—men tread the same round. Not only the wise, the brave or the unfortunate, but even the fastidious might well wish to die.'[21] The bored pleasure seeker and the philosopher might be nearer to one another than they thought, both seeking a release from the tedious repetitions of life, as Seneca seems to recognize elsewhere,

when, after condemning the desire for death that arises merely
from boredom, he admits that we may slip into this attitude
as a result of philosophy.[22]

Though the philosophy which he preached was a stern one
Seneca had a sensitive humanity which modified the harsher
features of Stoicism. The Stoics, he says in one of his works,
are thought to be hard, but in fact none are really kinder and
more devoted to mankind than they. Though the wise man will
not feel pity, he will show clemency, which, Seneca explains,
differs from pity as religion differs from superstition. He will
help others, not from emotion, but because of the bond that
unites mankind, and of all virtues none is more becoming to a
man than clemency.[23] Among human beings are to be counted
slaves. They are slaves; no, they are human beings; *servi sunt*;
immo homines.[24] It may be lawful to do anything to a slave,
but there are some things which the common law of living
things forbid one to do against a man, since he is a creature
of the same nature as oneself.[25] 'Treat your inferiors', writes
Seneca, 'as you would wish your superiors to treat you. Whenever you think what you are allowed to do to a slave, think
too that your master would be able to do the same to you.'[26]

But kindly and humane though he was, Seneca did not like
his fellow men, at any rate in the mass. He describes how he
went to a gladiatorial show, and came back a worse man, more
cruel and inhumane because he had been among men.[27] As he
looks round on society he sees much to arouse his distaste and
indignation. If a wise man, he says, should be angry at baseness
and crime, he would be perpetually angry. Whenever he leaves
home he will meet with criminals, with the avaricious, the
prodigal and the shameless. There are as many vices as there
are men. Society is like a concourse of wild beasts.[28] He cannot
find any encouragement in the hope of being able to improve
or reform his fellow men. His morality is essentially self-
centred, and he shrinks from degrading contacts. His advice to
Lucilius is to avoid crowds and to retire into himself, to mix
only with those likely to make him better or to be made better
by him.[29]

But if life was dismal and depressing, there was always the

thought of death to console one, death that was the end of all
the miseries of life. How ignorant of their own ills, he exclaims,
are those who do not praise death as the best invention of
nature. 'In death no one feels his lowliness; death obeys
none. . . . Death ensures that birth is not a punishment; it
causes me not to succumb to the threats of disaster, enables me
to preserve my mind intact and master of itself.'[30] And the way
to death was always open.

St Augustine criticized the Stoics for their inconsistency in
commending suicide while placing the highest good in this
life.[31] Yet Seneca's attitude was not altogether illogical. To him
it was the ultimate test of one's indifference to life that one
should be able to leave it; to those who said that one should
await the end that nature had decreed it could be answered
that they were derogating from man's freedom. 'In nothing
is the eternal law better vindicated than by the fact that it has
given us one entry to life but many ways of departure. . . . This
is the only ground on which we can make no complaint of life,
that it keeps nobody.'[32] But Seneca's justification of suicide was
perhaps ultimately based on other than purely intellectual
grounds. 'For nothing', he writes, 'is it more necessary to prepare
ourselves than for death. Other acts of preparation may prove
superfluous. We are prepared against poverty, and our riches
have held out. We have armed ourselves to despise pain, and,
having enjoyed sound limbs and good health, have never been
required to test this virtue. We have schooled ourselves to suffer
bereavement bravely, and fortune has preserved our loved ones
unharmed. But for death at least we shall not have practised in
vain, and the day will come when we shall be put to the test.'[33]
Here Seneca seems to speak of his own feelings. His life, apart
from his exile, had not been a hard one. He had not been
seriously tested, and felt perhaps some sense of guilt that this
was so. But there remained the final test, that of death, and if
he proved equal to this he might thereby atone for a life which
was unworthy of the philosophy he professed.

Seneca lived a life of uneasy compromise. The contrast
between his praises of poverty and his own riches was notorious,
and his professed desire to prove his virtue might provoke the

question whether there was not scope enough in public life under
Nero With his supple, ingenious mind, his ready sensibility
and his self-admiring cleverness he was in some ways ill cast
for the role of moral teacher, and something of the strained
atmosphere of a decadent age clings to his writings. It is with
a certain relief that one turns to men less gifted intellectually
but of simpler and sturdier character, Musonius and Epictetus.

If Seneca is the court preacher of Stoicism, Musonius is the
honest missionary, single-minded and thick-skinned, cheerful
in adversity, preaching in season and out of season. He is the
least intellectual of philosophers, a popularizer with a simple
message. For him philosophy teaches to avoid evil and attain
to virtue, and to be good is the same as to be a philosopher.[34]
All are capable of attaining to virtue. What is required is to
learn that death, hardship and poverty are not ills, and by
practice and discipline to overcome pleasure, ambition and
luxury.

Though he has no claim to be an original thinker, some of
Musonius's themes were unusual in the Rome of his day. His
belief that both sexes were equally capable of virtue was a part
of the Greek philosophical tradition of which little had been
heard in Rome.[35] His praise of marriage and large families is
different in spirit from the normal attitude of the Stoics, who,
while somewhat coldly recommending the duty of marriage,
tended to look on domestic ties as an unwelcome distraction.[36]
Most novel is his commendation of farming as a suitable
occupation for a philosopher.[37] His picture of the philosopher
living a hardy life of toil on the land and instructing his pupils
in moments of leisure is an incongruous mixture of the tradition
of the Greek philosophic teacher with the old Roman idealiza-
tion of peasant life. It is hard to imagine it ever being put into
effect.

Epictetus, though of Greek origin, belongs to Rome, for he
learned his philosophy from Musonius, taught in Rome before
his banishment and drew pupils from Rome when he moved
across the Adriatic. He was a man whose philosophy had been
tested by experience. He had been a slave, and had learned
from slavery a combination of independence and submission,

independence as regards essentials and submission in all else. For him what is fundamental is the distinction between what is under our control and what is not; what is under our control is the moral purpose, what is not is everything else. The former we must cultivate to the best of our ability; the latter is a matter of indifference. So man is freed from all encumbrances; he holds to what is truly his own, and secure in the knowledge of what is his, he can meet death, exile and imprisonment cheerfully. Events such as these only affect man's body or his property, and these are not the man himself.[38] The free man for Epictetus is the man who is subject to no restraints; and in order to be subject to no restraints one must be ready to abandon everything that can be affected by the action of others. The criterion to be applied to everything is whether it falls within the sphere of the moral purpose. What others do to us, being independent of our free choice, is nothing to us. We should therefore accept it, not wishing to change the constitution of things but rather keeping our wills in harmony with what happens.[39]

Epictetus lived through the reign of Domitian and his references to imprisonment, death and the tyrant's threats remind us that his teaching had a direct reference to the times in which he lived. But though the perils of despotism gave point to his message, it did not depend solely on the circumstances of his day or his position in life. His philosophy was essentially the same as that which half a century or so later sustained Marcus Aurelius, who, as ruler of the Roman world, had no tyrant to fear and nothing against which to arm himself except the ordinary annoyances of life and the temptations of power.

In Marcus Aurelius the Stoic self-discipline is found in its most refined form. There is none of the forced heroism of Seneca; instead we find an almost anxious striving after simplicity and sincerity. The basis of his thought is the belief that man must be true to himself, that is to the highest part of himself, the governing element, the deity within him. As this is a part of universal nature, man does violence to himself if he separates himself from nature and turns against what comes to pass instead of joyfully accepting it. He is untrue to himself if he allows himself to be affected by pleasure or pain, if he acts a part or does anything false, and if he behaves without plan or consistency.

Finally, man's true nature forbids him to turn against any other human being. Man violates his soul when he 'turns away from any human being or is borne against him with intent to injure him'.[40] 'Love the human race', he writes.[41] Yet this was a precept which he must have found it hard to live up to. Stoicism was not a gospel of love. The good Stoic would not be angry with others, for he knew they could not harm him and his reason told him they were his kinsmen. But the best of Stoics hardly loved his fellow men. Marcus Aurelius, as good a Stoic as could be, found it hard to put up with even the most attractive of his household; the men he met were, in his words, 'inquisitive, ungrateful, violent, treacherous, envious, uncharitable', and though his intellect told him they were his fellow men, his heart hardly felt it. One of the consolations of death on which he dwelt was that his soul would no longer be contaminated by the company of others. 'You should not be offended with them but care for them, bear them gently; yet they are not like-minded with you and death will bring a release from such.'[42]

Marcus Aurelius is the last of the Roman Stoics. After him the philosophy which had exercised so compelling an attraction for several centuries faded away. Its influence in after years was on the whole small. It had depended on a series of teachers whose life and example inspired as much as their words, and when the line of teachers came to an end Stoicism passed into history. In the fourth century, when Platonism was the predominant philosophy, the Stoics, with the Epicureans, were, according to Augustine, known only from the school teaching of the rhetoricians.[43]

But if Stoicism failed to survive, it had at least left its mark on Roman life as no other philosophy had. From the second century B.C. to the second century A.D. it had guided the lives of many Romans and influenced many more who would not have called themselves Stoics. Whereas the Greek Stoics were for the most part men of the study and the lecture room, writers and teachers, or at the best advisers of politicians, the Roman Stoics were rather men of affairs, closely concerned with the business of government. It would be hard to parallel in the Greek world the lives of such men as Rutilius Rufus and Cato, Thrasea, Helvidius Priscus and Marcus Aurelius. *Quantum enim Graeci praeceptis valent, tantum Romani, quod est maius, exemplis.* Quintilian's words[44] might well be applied to the history of the Stoa.

XII

HUMANITAS

THE STOICS, as we have seen, put forward an ideal based on the assumption that man was distinguished from other living creatures by the possession of reason and that he was therefore most truly himself when he cultivated the reasoning faculty to the exclusion of any other. There was, however, another ideal for man, based on a somewhat different view of his nature, which, though it was never precisely formulated, was of very real influence among the Romans. It is best exemplified in Cicero and best described by that favourite word of his, *humanitas*.

A few centuries after Cicero's day Aulus Gellius tried to explain the meaning of this word. *Humanitas*, he says, did not originally have the meaning which is now commonly assigned to it, namely, what the Greeks call φιλανθρωπία, an adaptability and general goodwill towards men, but by *humanitas* was meant more or less what the Greeks called παιδεία, and we learning and education in the liberal arts.[1] The explanation is correct up to a point. Ciceronian *humanitas* is παιδεία, but it is more than that; it is φιλανθρωπία also. The two aspects of the word together form a single concept, a single human ideal.

Among the qualities comprehended in the Ciceronian idea of *humanitas* are kindliness, helpfulness and consideration for others. Thus Cicero asks for Appius's help *pro tua singulari humanitate*; 'all my hopes', he writes to Atticus, 'of alleviating this unpleasantness rest *in tua humanitate*.'[2] *Humanitas* is joined with *clementia* and *mansuetudo*; it is contrasted with *severitas*.[3] The word also implies tolerance, politeness, easy manners and the social graces generally; witty and polished conversation, says Cicero in *De Oratore*, belong essentially to *humanitas*.[4] It was a quality which did not perhaps of itself comprehend the whole of the human virtues, for it did not include the sterner side of man's character displayed in action and political activity; when Cicero wished to praise a man in public he would refer not only to his *humanitas* (if he possessed this quality) but to his *virtus* also.[5] As for *gravitas*, that famous Roman virtue, this was hardly consistent with *humanitas*; Atticus is praised for having achieved in his life and speech an extremely difficult combination, that of these two qualities.[6]

In many passages of Cicero *humanitas* inclines rather to the other meaning, what Gellius called 'learning and education in the liberal arts'. The liberal arts, the ἐγκύκλιος παιδεία of the Greeks, are described as the arts devised to enable the minds of the young to be formed to *humanitas* and *virtus*.[7] We meet with such phrases as *doctrina aliqua et humanitate digna scientia, communes litterae et politior humanitas* and *studia humanitatis ac litterarum*. Scipio Aemilianus and the men of his circle who associated with cultured Greeks are described as *humanitate politi*.[8] It is the theme of Crassus in the first book of *De Oratore* that *humanitas*, in the sense of culture or education, is a requisite of the ideal orator, whereas Antonius takes the opposite view. In the second day's conversation Antonius is found to have changed his mind, and his conversion is welcomed with the significant words, 'the night has educated you and made you a man'. Antonius himself later on emphasizes the point when he remarks that it is the mark of a beast not of a man to shut one's ears to the teaching of the Greeks.[9]

It must not be supposed that for Cicero the two aspects of *humanitas* were as clearly distinguished as they are to us, or were to Gellius. Cicero regarded education as having an effect on the character; the liberal arts civilized a man and made him into a true man. Even the most evil character could be humanized by education.[10] A humane man in one sense should be humane in the other. 'It is the part not only of a great man and one by nature temperate, but also of one educated in learning and liberal studies, to wield the great power he has in such a way that those under him want no other rule.'[11] Humanism implies humaneness.

There is a famous line of Terence, *homo sum, humani nil a me alienum puto*.[12] It is spoken by a character who ventures to remonstrate with a neighbour with whom he is not intimately acquainted, and is told to mind his own business. The answer is that he is a man, and everything that concerns a man is his business. The idea implied is that men are united to one another by the common bond of humanity and that this should guide them in their attitude to one another. The idea was a Stoic one, though the tolerant, sympathetic attitude to mankind which Terence based on it was hardly derived from Stoicism. But whatever its origins, the belief in the common humanity of mankind naturally gives rise to the Ciceronian idea that kindliness, sympathy and tolerance are among the peculiar qualities of man. But if this is the basis of the Ciceronian ideal, its refinements belong rather to a sophisticated, urban civilization with agreed standards of behaviour and an appreciation of ease and polish in social relations and wit and style in conversation. 'Our conversation . . .', writes Cicero, 'should be good-natured, without stubbornness and seasoned with wit. The speaker should not monopolize the conversation to the exclusion of others, but as in other matters so here, should think it right that each man should have his turn.'[13] Something of this spirit appears in the Ciceronian dialogues, where the clash of controversy is muted by the civilities of a well-bred company discoursing in comfortable leisure. Dignified, well-mannered, good-humoured and lively conversation was something that the Romans appreciated. Parties, in Cicero's view, were not mere occasions for eating and drinking; they were *convivia*, a significant word, according to Cicero, pointing as it did to the purpose of such parties. They involved living together, and in company men lived in the truest sense.[14]

If the impression we get from Cicero is of a society polished and aristocratic, a *humanitas* confined to a narrow circle, flourishing only in a background of luxurious country villas, we should none the less remember that it was a society which, while it valued the social graces, valued also the things of the mind, and was prepared to accept the educated man, whatever his social background, as one who fulfilled the human ideal in

virtue of his education. The minor poet Archias and the young
slave Alexis could be classed among the *humani*.[15]

That literary attainments and culture generally should be
regarded as a part of the essential quality of the human being
may at first sight be somewhat unexpected, since such accomplishments can hardly be, and were not in Cicero's day, shared
by all mankind. They were, however, peculiar to man, and
could be regarded as characteristic of man in his highest form.
Though, says Cicero, the word 'man' is applied to everyone, it
belongs properly only to those who are educated in the arts
proper to mankind. He records a saying attributed doubtfully
to Plato, who when driven by a storm to an unknown land
observed some geometrical figures inscribed on the sand, and
told his companions to be of good cheer, because he saw the
traces of man.[16] No less significant is Cicero's comment. The
traces of man, he says, were found not in the cultivation of the
land, which was also to be seen, but in the signs of education.
Others have seen the essence of man in the capacity to make
things, and have contemplated with pride his achievements in
creating material civilization. To Cicero what distinguished
man from the beasts, and man in the highest sense from those
who had not developed man's fullest capacities, was intellectual
achievement.

It would be foolish to argue that because the Greeks had no
word corresponding to the Latin *humanitas* they lacked the
quality. The elder Pliny indeed praised Rome for having given
humanitas to mankind,[17] but his son by adoption knew better.
To the younger Pliny Greece was the original home of *humanitas*
and its inhabitants were *homines maxime homines*.[18] The
various aspects of Roman *humanitas* can be traced back to
Greece. Terence owed much to Menander; the belief in the
common bond uniting mankind was primarily a Stoic one. The
high value set on education and culture came from the Greek
world with the Greek teachers who passed on their accomplishments to the Romans, and the anecdote of Plato referred to
above is, of course, of Greek origin.[19] What the Greeks did
not do was to use a single word to denote the various
qualities included in the Latin word *humanitas*; they did

not use ἀνθρωπότης or ἀνθρωπισμὸς for φιλανθρωπία and παιδεία.

But though we may trace its constituent qualities back to Greece, there remains something un-Greek about Ciceronian *humanitas*. It is partly the external setting; the society centred in the town, but with its roots in the country; the wealth and comfort and self-confidence of a governing class; the practical ability and close contact with affairs. All this makes us feel when we read, for instance, the letters of Cicero, or even his philosophical treatises, that we are in a different world from that of the Greeks. And the external circumstances affect the Roman's outlook on life. For all his respect for intellectual pursuits as a part of *humanitas*, he remains at bottom a little sceptical about the intellect, unwilling to follow an argument to its logical conclusion and averse from the outlook of the professional teacher. However learned the Roman may be, he does not like to show off his learning, but prefers to pose as an amateur, a plain man, *unus paterfamilias* or *unus e togatis*.[20] The characters in Cicero's dialogues are made to show a reluctance to hold forth on a serious subject, a fear of being tedious or appearing professional. Piso in *De Finibus* is afraid of being *molestus* if he speaks about philosophy, Velleius in *De Natura Deorum* and Antonius in *De Oratore* apologize for being too long.[21] Cicero himself at the beginning of one of his philosophical works claims to be a mere Roman approaching his subject with diffidence.[22] Professional teachers were apt to argue in season and out of season and to bore and offend their listeners by their lack of tact. Such conduct the Romans branded with the word *ineptus*, and held the Greeks to be particularly prone to it.[23] Rome has now grown to maturity socially, and can give Greece lessons in behaviour.

While, as we have seen, the idea of *humanitas*, or at least its constituent elements, came to Rome from Greece, it was from Greece that there also came the most serious attacks on it. They came from the philosophers, insisting on the one thing necessary and rejecting all else as frivolous and distracting. Most radical of all were the Cynics, who stripped man of all inessentials and left him clothed only in the rags of the mendicant, with no

home but a tub, and no possessions but his moral independence.
The Cynics defied the conventions and despised the amenities
of life; they rejected the arts and accomplishments, literature,
music, mathematics and so on, as useless and unnecessary.[24]
Diogenes, we are told, 'marvelled that the teachers of literature
investigated the ills of Odysseus but knew nothing of their own;
that the musicians tuned the strings of their lyres while the
disposition of their souls was out of tune; that the astronomers
looked up to the sun and moon but neglected what was at their
feet; that the rhetoricians claimed to care for justice but did not
act in accordance with it'.[25] While the Cynics were most extreme
in their rejection of human culture, the Stoics sometimes came
near to them. Zeno had begun as a pupil of the Cynics, and
there was always a radical wing of Stoicism which came near
to Cynicism. Those who held that virtue was the sole good and
all else was indifferent might well ignore the graces of social
life and depreciate the intellectual and literary accomplishments
that did not contribute to virtue.

Poetry in particular was the old enemy of philosophy. For
poetry often conflicts with a strict morality. Plato excluded
the poets from his ideal state, and the same attitude of disapproval is found in later moralists. Even Cicero, writing under
the influence of the more radical philosophers, found himself
at times taking sides against poetry. The poets wrote of their
own and others' love affairs, and love, at any rate in some of
its manifestations, was one of the irrational emotions from
which the wise man must be free. They showed brave men
lamenting, and the truly brave man should be free from all
such weakness. They corrupted and enervated their readers, and
we, exclaims Cicero scornfully, taught by Greece, read and
learn all this and think it a liberal education.[26]

These remarks, however, only reflect a passing mood. Against
them we may quote the famous words in the speech for Archias:
'Even if pleasure alone were the object of learning, you must
acknowledge this to be the most humane and liberal exercise
of the mind. Other pursuits depend on particular times, ages or
places; but these studies give stimulus in youth and amusement
in old age; they grace prosperity and provide support and

solace in adversity; they delight at home and are no impediment abroad; they 'accompany us at night time, on our travels and in the country.'[27] We may refer too to the numerous passages in his letters and elsewhere which show Cicero a true man of letters. He writes to his friends that he is 'feeding on a library' or 'devouring literature', or that he has returned to his 'old friends, his books'; when a freedman of his had arranged the books in one of his villas he felt that the house 'had now acquired a soul'.[28] Numerous quotations and allusions show that his mind was well stored with literature, Greek and Latin. The most abiding influence on him was that of the study of literature and rhetoric and the belief which he imbibed in early life in the civilizing influence of such studies. We have already referred to that passage in his earliest extant work in which he made oratory the power which had brought man from barbarism to civilization. He later learned from philosophy that it was not so much speech as reason that made man what he was, but he knew that $\lambda \acute{o} \gamma o \varsigma$ included the power of speech as well as of thought, and his phrase *ratio et oratio* brought together the two aspects into one human ideal and united the mutually antagonistic disciplines of the philosopher and the rhetorician.[29]

Cicero, then, was first and foremost a man of letters, and he never forgot it, even when he was writing about philosophy. Even the *Tusculans,* where Cicero seems most ready to turn away from his old interests, open with a severe attack on those who neglect the literary graces. 'It may be that a man thinks aright but cannot express what he thinks elegantly; but to commit one's thoughts to writing without being able to arrange or adorn them or charm the reader with some degree of enjoyment is an impertinent misuse of leisure and literature.'[30] In the series of philosophical works we are reminded more than once that philosophical discussion serves as an exercise in speaking as well as a means of discovering the truth, and when we read the preface to *De Officiis* we begin to wonder whether philosophy to Cicero was anything more than a branch of literature. What he really prides himself on, so he writes, is not so much his knowledge of philosophy as his literary style. There were plenty of others who knew as much philosophy as he did; but none who could write so clearly and elegantly. The young Cicero, to whom the treatise is addressed, is recommended to read his father's philosophical works; as for the matter, he could judge for himself, but at any rate they would improve his style.[31] When Cicero attempted to console himself in the distress of mind that followed his daughter's death, he even persuaded himself that a liberal education was part of the qualification for entering the company of the gods after death and assuming a divine nature. 'Those who are pure, chaste, unimpaired and uncorrupt,' he wrote, 'those educated in the studies of good learning, lightly and easily fly to the gods, that is, to a nature like their own', and he assigns to Tullia a place in heaven as 'the best and most accomplished (*doctissimam*) of her sex'.[32]

The *humanitas* of Cicero and his circle passed away with the society of the late Republic. Yet something of the same spirit can be found under the Empire. The same love of letters, the same kindliness and tolerance are to be seen in the younger Pliny, though without Cicero's liveliness of mind and breadth of interest. Unlike Cicero, Pliny viewed philosophy with a respectful indifference, and his culture was confined to the relatively narrow sphere of literature and rhetoric. Literature was an absorbing interest to him, the chief of pleasures, a solace in distress and a bond between friends. 'A man', he writes, after urging a friend to visit Rome in order to hear the rhetorician Isaeus, 'must be quite lacking in taste and letters, indolent and I might almost say base, who will not make sacrifices for a study than which none is more entertaining, more noble and, finally, more humane.'[33] *Humanitas* for Pliny, as for Cicero, comprised not only literary interests, but kindliness—it is the quality which impels him to treat his slaves well and overwhelms him with distress when they fall sick—and tolerance and forgiveness. It tempers severity with geniality, and allows of pleasantry, harmless relaxation and even mild impropriety.[34]

The philosophers for their part had little use for literary pursuits, or indeed for any activity which did not lead to moral improvement. The spirit of Diogenes lived on in the Stoics of the Empire. Intent on the cultivation of what they considered the highest faculty in man, they ignored his other faculties; literary and artistic creation, the pursuit of knowledge, discovery and invention were at best irrelevant to the true aim of life, the pursuit of virtue.

In one of his letters Seneca gives his considered views on the liberal arts.[35] They are useful, he says, but only as preparation to the mind, not as its permanent occupation. There is only one truly liberal study, one, that is, which makes man free, philosophy. Other studies are suited only to the young. We should not study them, but rather have studied them.[36] Seneca proceeds to review the various arts of the ancient world. First he takes the art of the *grammaticus*, the teacher of language and literature. This study, he says, does not rid one of fear, desire or passion. What is the use of investigating the relative age of Homer and Hesiod or the various problems raised by the interpretation of Homer? It is more important to teach how to live aright. Music, mathematics and astronomy are similarly depreciated. To the musician Seneca says: 'Rather teach my soul to be in harmony with itself', and to the mathematician: 'Measure me the mind of man'; while the astronomer (or astrologer) has nothing to teach the Stoic, who awaits the future with a serene mind, prepared for any event. Painting, sculpture and other such arts Seneca dismisses as simply aids to luxury.

Nor does he regard the invention of useful techniques as a source of pride to man.[37] He takes Posidonius to task for ascribing to philosophy the invention of houses, weaving, agriculture and other crafts. These, he says, were the work of man, but not of the wise man. The philosophy which taught man to reduce his wants to a minimum and live as simply as possible had no use for the refinements of life, and looked on improvements in technique as merely adding to the superfluous baggage which a wise man would dispense with. How, asks Seneca, can one consistently admire both Diogenes and Daedalus? Craftsmen are unnecessary; it is enough to follow nature.

The same indifference to culture is found in Epictetus. He
was a follower of Diogenes with no admiration for Daedalus,
prepared to dismiss the Acropolis as 'bits of stone and a pretty
rock'. For him reading is of no use unless it produces serenity.
Athens may be beautiful, but happiness is much more so.[38]
Always morality comes first. Not that Epictetus regarded
culture with enmity. He does not despise faculties other than
the moral, and is more favourable to rhetoric than some
rhetoricians were to philosophy.[39] But he certainly had no
personal interest in liberal culture.

It was otherwise with Marcus Aurelius. He had had a
thorough education in rhetoric and was by nature a bookish
man. His conversion to philosophy meant a deliberate abandonment of other interests. He had learned from Rusticus to 'turn
his back on rhetoric and poetry and clever speech', and has to
urge himself to 'put away his books' or 'cast aside his thirst
for books'.[40] Everything must be seen as it is, analysed into
its constituent parts and reduced to the matter of which it is
formed; and Marcus applies the same relentless analysis to the
pleasures of eye and ear as to those of food and sex. 'The
rottenness of the matter which underlies everything, water,
dust, bones, stench. Marble—incrustation of earth; gold and
silver—sediments; dress—hair of animals; purple dye—blood,
and so on.' Music too, he notes, will be despised, if it is analysed
into its constituents.[41] Nothing must be allowed to attain too
great a hold over him or distract him from his austere devotion
to reason.

While philosophy led the Stoics of the Empire to turn their
backs on liberal culture, the professed upholders of that culture
were now men like Marcus Aurelius's old tutor, Fronto, worthy
lovers of letters, proud of their accomplishments, but far
removed from the spirit of Cicero. The characteristic Roman
figure of the cultured, genial, tolerant man of affairs has passed
away, and we are left with the rhetorician, the professional
teacher, with his somewhat narrow conception of culture,
excessively concerned with the technique of fine writing and
oblivious to or resentful of philosophy. In Fronto there is the
old pride in literary culture, but pedantry and professionalism

have crept in; παιδεία has prevailed over *humanitas*. Yet there is still that union of friendship with literary culture which is so characteristic of Roman humanism. 'My love of Cornelianus Sulpicius', writes Fronto, 'sprang from delight at his character and his eloquence, for he is highly gifted in the latter respect, and I cannot deny that what I value most is friendship based on culture.' 'By culture,' he adds, 'I mean that of the rhetoricians; that is, I feel, somehow human, whereas that of the philosophers is divine.'[42]

XIII

EPILOGUE

THE DEVELOPMENT of Roman culture, as was pointed out at the beginning of this study, was the result of Rome's conquest of the Hellenistic world and her absorption and adaptation of its thought and literature. There was, however, one people in the Eastern Mediterranean which, though included within the sphere of Hellenistic civilization, remained only partially influenced by it, and retained a strong individuality and national consciousness. The Jews refused to be absorbed by Rome, and Rome refused to learn from them. But out of Judaism there came Christianity, the last and greatest spiritual movement of the ancient world, which was to prove a more powerful influence than any of the philosophies of Greece, and was to supersede both the religion and the philosophy of the Roman world in a new synthesis of religion and philosophy, and, one might almost say, supersede, through the institution of the Church, the Roman state itself.

The story of the spread of Christianity to Rome is very different from that of the spread of Greek philosophy. The opposition which the Greeks encountered in the second century before Christ was slight, and it was not long before they were accepted and welcomed as honoured masters, whereas Christianity had to contend for long against distrust, dislike and active persecution. And as the struggle was longer and more severe, so the conquest was more complete. Captive Greece, as Horace had said, took captive her fierce conqueror. Rome also conquered, indeed annihilated, Judaea; once more the captive proved conqueror in the end. The victory of Christianity meant a transformation of thought and society more thorough than anything achieved by Greek philosophy.

To describe in detail this transformation is not our purpose.

But something will be said by way of epilogue to indicate how much of the various movements which we have followed through the classical period survived into Latin Christianity.

Of the specifically Roman tradition, the spirit of patriotism, the sense of history and the admiration for the great men of the past, little survived. How little, is shown in striking fashion by the fact that both Ambrose and Lactantius use the famous phrase *maiores nostri* not of those old Romans on whom Cicero had loved to dwell, but of the Jewish heroes.[1] Roman patriotism had always been closely linked with Roman religion; for the Christians service to the state meant service to paganism and the worship of an emperor they could not worship. Roman power was accepted as a source of stability, but without enthusiasm. The martial tradition, once a source of pride, became the object of condemnation, and the history of Rome was rewritten not as a glorious epic of the triumph of manly virtue, but as a sordid story of robbery and violence. Rome, said the pagans, owed her empire to her piety. On the contrary, the Christians replied, conquest meant spoliation of other peoples' gods, and the Romans had grown great not by piety, but by unpunished sacrilege.[2] Augustine, looking back on the history of Rome after the sack of the capital, sees the Roman state as inspired mainly by lust for power, *libido dominandi*.[3] Lactantius can prophesy, though not without a shudder of horror at the prospect, the end of Roman power, and Augustine can so far withdraw himself from the world in which he lived as to contemplate its actual end with an impartial detachment.[4]

Of Roman religion, officially at least, nothing survived in the new Latin Christian civilization. The Christians had their own religion, and they refused to compromise with others. Unlike other religions theirs had the support of theology, and theology had developed from philosophy. Thus we find the Christian Fathers sometimes joining hands with the pagan philosophers and repeating their arguments and their attitudes. In their attacks on polytheism and the cults of the pagans they found much that they could borrow from in the long tradition of philosophic criticism. They can even claim to be the champions of reason against blind acceptance of tradition. 'So great', writes

Lactantius, 'is the authority of antiquity that they say it is a crime to inquire into it', but 'each man should trust in himself and rely on his own judgment.'[5] The Christians were indeed the inheritors of pagan philosophy rather than of pagan religion, and they drew from philosophy not only their method but many of their arguments. A liberal Christian like Minucius Felix could expound his religion in terms hardly distinguishable from those of non-Christian theism, and after a survey of Greek philosophy could remark: 'One would think that either present-day Christians were philosophers or old philosophers were Christians.'[6]

In the final development of Latin Christianity in the fourth century Platonism was the most important philosophic influence, and the Stoicism that had been so congenial to the Romans in earlier centuries contributed little. Augustine met with no Stoics in his spiritual pilgrimage. There was, however, one part of Stoic doctrine which passed into Christian theology, the idea of a providence ordaining all for the benefit of mankind. Here the distinctive Christian doctrine of creation modified the Stoic theory. Whereas the Stoics combined a belief in providence with an identification of God with nature, to the Christian providence suggested rather a divine being external to nature, creator and governor of all things, but not identified with the objects of his creation and governance. As Lactantius put it: 'If the world was constructed, it must presumably be constructed as a house or ship is, in which case there is some divine artificer of the world, and the world which is made is something separate from him who made it.'[7]

To Minucius Felix the main difference between the Christians and the philosophers was not that their ideals were different, but that the Christians succeeded in living up to their ideals whereas the philosophers did not.[8] Yet there were differences between the ideals of Christianity and those of philosophy, if by philosophy is meant Stoicism. The Christians could, of course, endorse much that the Stoics had taught, and could on occasion quote admiringly from their writings. But the differences between the two creeds are more fundamental than their resemblances. Unlike Christianity, Stoicism was a creed for the few; though it acknowledged in theory that all men were possessed of reason and capable of goodness, in practice it demanded a degree of self-control and self-cultivation that was beyond the reach of most men. It could never attract the multitude, and its poor relation Cynicism, intellectually weaker, but better able to appeal to the many, survived when Stoicism itself decayed.[9] Not only were the Stoics exacting in their moral demands; they also relied solely on precept and example, developed no organization or common life, rejected the aids of myth and cult, and offered no rewards but the consciousness of right. As Pascal said, they knew man's duty but not his weakness.[10] They believed that man could attain to wisdom by his own intellect and virtue by his own effort, whereas to the Christian knowledge of the truth depends on revelation and man requires the help of grace.

Like other pagan systems of philosophy, Stoicism set the *summum bonum* in this life. The Stoics looked to the attainment of happiness or blessedness, and though they rejected the commonly accepted goods of life, they held that virtue produced happiness and was of itself sufficient to do so. This had always been hard to accept. As we have seen, Cicero was at times oppressed by the thought that the human mind no less than the human body might be by nature too weak to attain to felicity, but to him the alternative was that man could not be the master but must be the slave of circumstances.[11] The Christian, admitting the ills and imperfections of this life and regarding them as inevitable in man's fallen state, looked to the attainment of felicity only in eternal life. Thus he was saved from the necessity of preserving man's dignity and belief in himself by denying that evil was evil and maintaining that man could be happy under torture.

The Stoic ideal of freedom from emotion met with little sympathy from the Christians. It had indeed been somewhat modified in the practice and teaching of later Stoicism, but it remained the doctrine of the school, and the criticisms of the Peripatetics and others had little effect. Among the Christians we find Lactantius robustly rejecting the Stoic view, holding that the emotions are natural, that it is both impossible and

undesirable to remove them, and that they should therefore
be directed into the right channels.[12] The argument is not
specifically Christian, but it is easy to see that a religion which
described God in terms of human emotion, and which regarded
the fear of God as the beginning of wisdom and the love of
God as man's first duty, would have little sympathy with the
ideal of ἀπάθεια.

But perhaps the greatest difference between Christianity and
Stoicism lies in their different conceptions of the relation of
man to god. To the Stoic man is akin to God by virtue of the
possession of reason, and can make himself equal to God by
the cultivation of the highest part of himself. As Epictetus put
it, the philosopher desires to become a god instead of a man.[13]
For the Christian on the other hand the words 'Ye shall be as
gods' were the words of the tempter and the origin of man's fall.

Stoicism, as has already been said, had ceased to be of much
importance in the age of the greatest Latin Christian writers.
There was, however, one voice from the Roman past which
was still living, that of Cicero. It might indeed be maintained
that Stoicism had more influence on Christianity through
Cicero than through any professed Stoic, for of all non-
Christian writings the second book of *De Natura Deorum* is
perhaps the one of which most echoes are found in the Latin
Fathers. *De Officiis* too was used, though admittedly with little
understanding, by St Ambrose as the basis for his manual for
the clergy, and Stoic ideas of justice and natural law found
their way into Christian thought through *De Republica* and
De Legibus. Most important of all perhaps, it was Cicero's
Hortensius, a work in which philosophy in general rather than
the philosophy of any one school was commended, that turned
Augustine's thoughts away from earthly things and set him
on the path which led to the Christian faith. It is indeed interesting to observe how after the comparative neglect of the
intervening years Cicero comes into his own again in the
Christian period. In an earlier chapter we noted that in the
early Empire the Stoic saint Cato proved more influential than
the scholarly Cicero. But the memory of saints survives only so
long as there exists a body of faithful followers to revere them,

whereas writers survive as long as they are read. When Roman Stoicism as a living school came to an end, the way was clear for Cicero, who had founded no school, to influence men by his books.

But though Cicero played his part in the *praeparatio evangelica*, he represented, for Jerome at any rate, as all who remember his famous dream will know, rather the antithesis of the Christian spirit. For Cicero was the idol of the rhetorical schools, the symbol of that literary culture whose vanities the true Christian rejected. This culture, as we have seen, had already been subjected to attacks from the philosophers, and the Christians followed them, pursuing the attack with greater vehemence, since the culture of the pagan world was so closely bound up with a religion which they rejected. But even in the early days of Latin Christian writing Tertullian's wholesale repudiation of secular studies is balanced by the sweet reasonableness and literary charm of Minucius Felix, writing in the style and the spirit of Cicero. The battle ended in the compromise of Augustine, by which secular studies were admitted as subordinate to sacred learning. On the face of it classical humanism was defeated.

But the official compromise hardly represented the real position. The humane studies of the Greco-Roman world survived, and were still felt to have a value independent of their uses in the interpretation of Scripture. The change of faith made little difference to the literary traditions of the later Empire; Christian poets wrote in the classical metres and Christian preachers followed in the steps of the pagan sophists. The study of literature and rhetoric was firmly established in the educational system of the Empire, and even when this system decayed with the decay of the Empire the idea of education which it represented survived. The classics were still read, and even when imperfectly understood were still regarded as classics. The humanism of the ancient world, though it might seem to rest on so weak an intellectual foundation, showed itself none the less one of the most enduring influences in later years. Churchmen might condemn the lies of the poet or the vanities of the orator, might prove to their satisfaction that man's sole duty on earth was the service of God and the preparation for eternal life, but the classics of Latin literature remained to remind mankind that life on this earth could be adorned and sweetened by the use of man's gifts for creation, study and social life. They preserved the memory of a people who had not only conquered and governed the world but had created a society which in its highest forms was considerate and tolerant, polished without formality, valuing friendship and sociability, respectful to learning and devoted to literature.

ABBREVIATIONS

Ad Her.	*Ad Herennium*
Ael.	Aelian
Var. Hist.	*Varia Historia*
Ambr.	St. Ambrose
Off. Min.	*De Officiis Ministrorum*
App. Verg.	*Appendix Vergiliana*
Cat.	*Catalepton*
Athen.	Athenaeus
Aug.	St. Augustine
C.D.	*De Civitate Dei*
Contr. Ac.	*Contra Academicos*
Cic.	Cicero
Ac. Post.	*Academica Posteriora*
Ac. Pr.	*Academica Priora*
Arch.	*Pro Archia*
Att.	*Ad Atticum*
Balb.	*Pro Balbo*
Brut.	*Brutus*
Caec.	*Pro Caecina*
Cael.	*Pro Caelio*
Cat.	*In Catilinam*
Cat. Maj.	*Cato Major (De Senectute)*
Clu.	*Pro Cluentio*
De Am.	*De Amicitia (Laelius)*
Deiot.	*Pro Rege Deiotaro*
De Or.	*De Oratore*
Div.	*De Divinatione*
Div. Caec.	*Divinatio in Caecilium*
Dom.	*De Domo*
Fam.	*Ad Familiares*
Fin.	*De Finibus*
Flacc.	*Pro Flacco*
Font.	*Pro Fonteio*
Har. Resp.	*De Haruspicum Responsis*
Hort.	*Hortensius*
Imp. Pomp.	*De Imperio Cn. Pompeii (Pro Lege Manilia)*
Inv.	*De Inventione*
Lael.	*Laelius (De Amicitia)*
Leg.	*De Legibus*
Leg. Agr.	*De Lege Agraria*
Lig.	*Pro Ligario*
Marc.	*Pro Marcello*
Mil.	*Pro Milone*
Mur.	*Pro Murena*

N.D.	*De Natura Deorum*
Off.	*De Officiis*
Or.	*Orator*
Parad.	*Paradoxa Stoicorum*
Phil.	*Philippica*
Pis.	*In Pisonem*
Planc.	*Pro Plancio*
Post Red. ad Quir.	*Post Reditum ad Quirites*
Post Red. in Sen.	*Post Reditum in Senatu*
Q.F.	*Ad Quintum Fratrem*
Quinct.	*Pro Quinctio*
Rab. Perd.	*Pro Rabirio Perduellionis Reo*
Rab. Post.	*Pro Rabirio Postumo*
Rep.	*De Republica*
Rosc. Am.	*Pro Roscio Amerino*
Sest.	*Pro Sestio*
Sull.	*Pro Sulla*
Tusc.	*Tusculanae Disputationes*
Vat.	*In Vatinium*
Verr.	*In Verrem*
C.I.L.	*Corpus Inscriptionum Latinarum*
Corn Nep.	Cornelius Nepos
Att.	*Atticus*
D.L.	Diogenes Laertius
Dio Chrys.	Dio Chrysostom
Enn.	Ennius
Scen.	*Scenica*
Epict.	Epictetus
Gell.	Gellius
Hist. Aug.	*Historia Augusta*
M. Ant.	*Marcus Antoninus*
Fronto	
Ad Ant. Pium	*Ad Antoninum Pium*
Ad M. Caes.	*Ad Marcum Caesarem*
Ad Verum Imp.	*Ad Verum Imperatorem*
Hor.	Horace
Ep.	*Epistles*
Epod.	*Epodes*
Sat.	*Satires*
Isocrates	
Ad Nic.	*Ad Nicoclem*
Lact.	Lactantius
Inst. Div.	*Institutiones Divinae*
Liv.	Livy
Luc.	Lucan
Lucr.	Lucretius
M. Ant.	Marcus Antoninus (Marcus Aurelius)
Min. Fel.	Minucius Felix
Oct.	*Octavius*
Mus.	Musonius

Ov.	Ovid
Am.	*Amores*
Ars Am.	*Ars Amatoria*
Fast.	*Fasti*
Met.	*Metamorphoses*
Trist.	*Tristia*
Ox. Pap.	*Oxyrrhynchus Papyri*
Pers.	Persius
Pet. Cons.	*De Petitione Consulatus*
Plat.	Plato
Phaed.	*Phaedo*
Tim.	*Timaeus*
Plin.	Pliny (elder)
N.H.	*Naturalis Historia*
Plin.	Pliny (younger)
Ep.	*Epistulae*
Pan.	*Panegyricus*
Plut.	Plutarch
Aem. Paul.	*Aemilius Paulus*
Cat. Maj.	*Cato Major*
Cat. Min.	*Cato Minor*
Crass.	*Crassus*
Pomp.	*Pompey*
Prof. Virt.	*De Profectu in Virtute*
Pol.	Polybius
Prop.	Propertius
Quint.	Quintilian
Sall.	Sallust
Jug.	*Jugurtha*
Sen.	Seneca (elder)
Contr.	*Controversiae*
Suas.	*Suasoriae*
Sen.	Seneca (younger)
Ben.	*De Beneficiis*
Brev.	*De Brevitate Vitae*
Clem.	*De Clementia*
Cons. Helv.	*Consolatio ad Helviam*
Cons. Marc.	*Consolatio ad Marciam*
Cons. Pol.	*Consolatio ad Polybium*
Const. Sap.	*De Constantia Sapientis*
Ep.	*Epistulae*
N.Q.	*Naturales Quaestiones*
Prov.	*De Providentia*
Tranqu.	*De Tranquillitate*
Vit. Beat.	*De Vita Beata*
Stoic. Vet. Frag.	*Stoicorum Veterum Fragmenta*
Suet.	Suetonius
Aug.	*Augustus*
Div. Jul.	*Divus Julius*
Gram.	*De Grammaticis*

Tac.	Tacitus
Agr.	*Agricola*
Ann.	*Annals*
Dial.	*Dialogus de Oratoribus*
Hist.	*Histories*
Ter.	Terence
Heaut.	*Heautontimorumenus*
Tert.	Tertullian
Apol.	*Apology*
Virg.	Virgil
Aen.	*Aeneid*
Ecl.	*Eclogues*
Georg.	*Georgics*
Vitr.	Vitruvius

NOTES

INTRODUCTION (pages 1 to 7)

¹ Pol. VI. 25, 11; cf. Cic. *Rep.* II. 30.
² Tac. *Dial.* 28; Plin. *Ep.* VIII. xiv, 4–6; Gwynn, *Roman Education*, ch. 1.
³ *C.I.L.* I. 2, 15.
⁴ Pol. XXXI. 23–4.
⁵ Pol. VI. 53, 9–10; cf. Sall. *Jug.* IV. 5.
⁶ Plin. *Ep.* VIII. xiv. 4–6.
⁷ Pol. VI. 56, 12–15.
⁸ ibid.
⁹ Plut. *Cat. Maj.* XX. 3; *Aem. Paul.* VI. 4–5.
¹⁰ Athen. XII. 547a; Ael. *Var. Hist.* 9, 12.
¹¹ Plut. *Cat. Maj.* xxii.
¹² See note 4.

CHAPTER I (pages 8 to 18)

¹ Sallust makes Marius refer with scorn to those *qui postquam consules facti sunt et acta maiorum et Graecorum militaria praecepta legere coeperint. Jug.* lxxxv. 12.
² Cic. *De Am.* 1, *Cael.* 10 f.
³ Cic. *Leg.* II. 59.
⁴ Cic. *De Or.* I. 166 f., 193–7.
⁵ Cic. *Ac. Post.* I. 9.
⁶ Cic. *Inv.* I. 35.
⁷ Cic. *Inv.* II. 159 f., *Ad Her.* III. 3 f.
⁸ Cic. *Inv.* III. 157, II. 160.
⁹ *Ad Her.* IV. 20, 24, 54 f.
¹⁰ *Ad Her.* III. 3.
¹¹ Cic. *Har. Resp.* 19, *Rosc. Am.* 131, *Dom.* 104, *Imp. Pomp.* 70, *Cael.* 59, *Cat.* I. 33, II. 19, *Dom.* 107.
¹² Cic. *Har. Resp.* 18–19.
¹³ Cic. *Cat.* II. 29, *Post Red. in Sen.* 2, *Dom.* 143, *Mil.* 83 f., *Cat.* III. 21, *Rab. Perd.* 5, *Cat.* I. 11, I. 33, III. 1, *Sull.* 40, 86.
¹⁴ Cic. *Mil.* 83 f.
¹⁵ Cic. *Dom.* 144, *Imp. Pomp.* 70, *Cat.* I. 33, *Sull.* 86, *Sest.* 45. In *Verr.* II. v. 184 f. other gods of non-Roman origin, whom Verres had offended, are added.
¹⁶ Cic. *Cat.* II. 29, III. 22.
¹⁷ Cic. *Post Red. in Sen.* 2, *Har. Resp.* 57, *Post Red. ad Quir.* 2, *Verr.* II. i. 112, *Planc.* 31. *Pietas: Planc.* 29; cf. *Rosc. Am.* 37, *Cael.* 3, *Div. Caec.* 61 f., *Mur.* 12.
¹⁸ Cic. *Cat.* I. 17, *Post Red. in Sen.* 1, *Post Red. ad Quir.* 4.
¹⁹ Cic. *Rab. Perd.* 33.
²⁰ Cic. *Sest.* 136–7.
²¹ Suet. *Div. Jul.* LXXVII.
²² Cic. *Rab. Perd.* 10, *Flacc.* 25, *Planc.* 60. Cf. *Dom.* 77, *Planc.* 33.

158 THE ROMAN MIND

23 Cic. *Rab. Post.* 22, *id.* 24.
24 Cic. *Leg. Agr.* II. 16, II. 29.   Cf. *id*. I. 21–2, *Verr.* II. v. 163, *Phil.*
VI. 19.
25 Cic. *Cat.* IV. 16, *Phil.* X. 20.
26 Cic. *Dom.* 33.
27 Cic. *Rosc. Am.* 50, *Cael.* 39.
28 Cic. *Flacc.* 28.
29 Cic. *Verr.* II. ii. 7, *Phil.* IX. 13, *Cael.* 33, *Clu.* 129, *Sest.* 6, 130, *Cael.* 39.
30 Cic. *Rosc. Am.* 111.
31 Cic. *Clu.* 5, 76, 107, *Div. Caec.* 8, *Verr.* II. iii. 210, v. 45.
32 Cic. *Rosc. Am.* 69, *Verr.* II. iv. 9, *Caec.* 34.
33 Cic. *Mur.* 17, *Rosc. Am.* 154, *Div. Caec.* 66, 69, *Leg. Agr.* I. 19.
34 Cic. *Leg. Agr.* II. 95.
35 Cic. *Cael.* 40, *Verr.* II. i. 56, *Div. Caec.* 70.
36 Cic. *Balb.* 15, *Flacc.* 15, *Verr.* II. iv. 115.
37 Cic. *Planc.* 62.
38 Cic. *Cael.* 39.
39 Cic. *Dom.* 39, *Balb.* 13, *Deiot.* 16, 37. *Virtus* and *gravitas*: *Quinct.* 5,
Imp. Pomp. 61, *Flacc.* 103, *Sest.* 60, *Sull.* 82. *Virtus* and *constantia*: *Imp. Pomp.*
68, *Sull.* 62; *gravitas* and *constantia*: *Font.* 24, *Sest.* 88, *Sull.* 83. *Magnitudo
animi* coupled with *gravitas* and *constantia*: *Deiot.* 37; with *gravitas*: *Planc.*
50, *Sest.* 141, *Mur.* 60; with *constantia*: *Sull.* 34, *Sest.* 26, *id.* 139.
40 *Fides*: *Quinct.* 5, *Verr.* I. 51, II. i. 4, ii. 4, *Mur.* 23, *id.* 30, *Sull.* 82,
Sest. 26, *Planc.* 3, *id.* 9, *Deiot.* 8, *id.* 16, *Caec.* 104. *Integritas*: *Verr.* I. 51,
II. i. 4, iv. 7, *Imp. Pomp.* 68, *Sest.* 60, *Caec.* 55, *Balb.* 9, *Planc.* 3, *id.* 9, *Deiot.*
16. *Frugalitas*: *Verr.* II. i. 137, v. 20, *Deiot.* 26 (where equated with *modestia*
and *temperantia* and described as the greatest of virtues). *Continentia*: *Verr.*
II. iii. 1, *Mur.* 23, *Arch.* 16, *Vat.* 26, *Planc.* 3, *id.* 9.   *Temperantia*: *Verr.* II.
iv. 81, *Font.* 40, *Imp. Pomp.* 13, *Mur.* 30, *id.* 60. *Moderatio*: *Font.* 40.
41 Cic. *Rab. Post.* 3, *Marc.* 9.
42 Cic. *Verr.* II. ii. 4, iv. 81.
43 Cic. *Imp. Pomp.* 13, *Rab. Perd.* 26, *Deiot.* 8.
44 Cic. *Mur.* 6, *Sull.* 1, *id.* 8, *Cat.* IV. 11.
45 Cic. *Rosc. Am.* 112, *Planc.* 80.
46 Cic. *Rosc. Am.* 111.
47 Cic. *Planc.* 5.
48 Cic. *Lig.* 38.
49 In *Phil.* XI. 28, however, patriotic action is said to belong to the law
sanctioned by Jupiter himself.
50 Cic. *Rosc. Am.* 67.
51 Cic. *Sest.* 47.
52 In *Sest.* 143 Cicero combines the idea of survival of the soul with
that of the immortality of fame.
53 Cic. *Post Red. in Sen.* 3; cf. *Vat.* 8, *Dom.* 86, *Rab. Post.* 42.
54 Cic. *Planc.* 90.
55 Cic. *Mil.* 97; cf. *Phil.* IX. 10, XIV. 33.
56 Cic. *N. D.* I. 6.
57 Cic. *Marc.* 19, *Phil.* XI. 28.
58 Epicureanism: Cic. *Post Red. in Sen.* 14, *Pis.* 68–72. Cato's Stoicism:
Mur. 61. Non-committal attitude: *Sest.* 47, *Deiot.* 37.

[59] Cic. *Rosc. Am.* 75.

[60] *Ad Her.* II. 34. The version given in the text is abbreviated from the original, which is given as an example of *vitiosa expositio quae nimium longe repetitur*.

[61] Compare Cic. *Sest.* 47–8 with *Ad Her.* IV. 54 f.

CHAPTER II (pages 19 to 31)

[1] Cic. *Ac. Pr.* II. 8.

[2] Cic. *Tusc.* II. 4.

[3] Cicero speaks of men's surprise that he had undertaken the defence *desertae disciplinae et iam pridem relictae* (*N. D.* I. 6). The reference is to the 'New' Academy. The revised version of Academicism popularized by Antiochus, allegedly a revival of the Old Academy, had Roman followers in Brutus, Varro and Piso.

[4] Cic. *Fin.* II. 44.

[5] Cic. *Tusc.* IV. 7.

[6] Cic. *Tusc.* IV. 6.

[7] Cic. *Fam.* XV. 19, 3–4.

[8] Cic. *Fin.* II. 119.

[9] Cic. *Tusc.* I. 10–11, *id.* 48.

[10] 'Towards the end of the Roman Republic faith in a future life was reduced to a minimum.' Cumont, *After Life in Roman Paganism*, p. 17.

[11] Lucr. V. 1453–5.

[12] Cic. *N. D.* II. 159.

[13] Cic. *Inv.* I. 2. Cf. the similar account in *Sest.* 91, there referred to as generally accepted.

[14] Cic. *Tusc.* V. 5.

[15] Lucr. V. 988–1010.

[16] Lucr. V. 1412 f.

[17] Lucr. V. 332 f.

[18] Lucr. V. 1456–7. Here, and elsewhere, I have borrowed from Bailey's translation.

[19] Lucr. VI. 9 f.

[20] D.L. X. 131–2.

[21] D.L. X. 6.

[22] Cic. *Fin.* II. 29–30.

[23] Cic. *Fin.* I. 37.

[24] Cic. *Fin.* I. 43–4, *id.* 46, Lucr. VI. 25.

[25] Cic. *Fin.* I. 59.

[26] D.L. X. 130–1.

[27] Lucr. II. 29 f.

[28] D.L. X. 118; Usener, *Epicurea*, 483.

[29] Usener, *Epicurea* 456, Cic. *Tusc.* V. 94.

[30] Horace, *Sat.* I. ii. 109 f. Philodemus: *id.* 121–2 (but Philodemus probably made this remark in an erotic poem rather than in an exposition of Epicureanism). Compare Horace's use of *parabilis* and *facilis* in l. 119 with *parabilis* in Cic. *Fin.* I. 45 and *facilis* in *Tusc.* V. 94.

[31] Lucr. IV. 1058 f. Contrast the Epicurean attitude expressed in *Tusc.* V. 94. Prescriptions for avoiding love: *Tusc.* IV. 74–5.

³² Compare Cercidas in *Ox. Pap.* 8.1082 with Lucr. IV. 1071, and note the Cynic ἀναίδεια of Lucretius's line 1065.

³³ Cic. *Fin.* I. 59.

³⁴ Lucr. II. 7–13.

³⁵ Lucr. V. 1129 f.

³⁶ Lucr. III. 1060 f.

³⁷ Cic. *Tusc.* V. 88–9.

³⁸ Cic. *Fin.* I. 71–2.

³⁹ Cic. *N. D.* I. 93.

⁴⁰ Lucr. I. 921–33.

⁴¹ Cic. *Fin.* I. 25–6.

⁴² Cic. *Brut.* 131, *Tusc.* V. 108.

⁴³ Tac. *Ann.* IV. 34.

CHAPTER III (pages 32 to 41)

¹ Cic. *Mur.* 61.

² Cic. *Tusc.* IV. 53. Cf. *Parad. Proem.* 4, where Cicero says that he personally accepts the paradoxes.

³ Pol. XXXI 24, 6–7.

⁴ Luc. II. 338–91.

⁵ Cic. *Fin.* I. 30.

⁶ *Stoic. Vet. Frag.* III. 640.

⁷ *Stoic. Vet. Frag.* III. 611. The Greek word πολιτεύεσθαι becomes *gerere et administrare rempublicam* in Cic. *Fin.* III. 68.

⁸ *Stoic. Vet. Frag.* I. 259, III. 738, Cic. *Fin.* III. 18.

⁹ Cic. *Off.* I. 113; See Pohlenz, *Die Stoa*, I. p. 201.

¹⁰ Cic. *Off.* I. 148.

¹¹ Cic. *N. D.* II. 87.

¹² Cic. *N. D.* II. 99.

¹³ Cic. *N. D.* II. 120–9.

¹⁴ Cic. *N. D.* II. 133.

¹⁵ Cic. *N. D.* II. 150 f.

¹⁶ Cic. *N. D.* II. 154 f.

¹⁷ Cic. *N. D.* II. 73.

¹⁸ Lucr. V. 195 f.

¹⁹ Lucr. V. 222 f.

²⁰ Cic. *N. D.* II. 151–2.

²¹ For the latter point see Cic. *Off.* II. 12–15.

²² Sen. *Ep.* XC. 7, 11, 12, 20–2.

²³ See Cic. *Div.* I. 116, *Leg.* I. 26.

CHAPTER IV (pages 42 to 53)

¹ Pol. VI. 43–4.

² Pol. VI. 11.

³ Pol. VI. 47; *id.* 9, 57.

⁴ Cic. *Rep.* I. 34.

⁵ Cic. *Rep.* VI. 1.

⁶ Cic. *Rep.* II. 1–2. Compare Burke on the British constitution: 'It is the result of the thoughts of many minds, in many ages.' *Appeal from the New to the Old Whigs. Works* (1883), III, p. 111.

[7] Pol. VI. 10, 12–14.

[8] This applies to the older Stoics. There were a few exceptions among later members of the school, such as Diogenes and Panaetius. Cic. *Leg.* III. 14.

[9] Cic. *Fin.* 63, *Off.* III. 27.

[10] Cic. *Fin.* III. 64.

[11] Cic. *Att.* II. 16, 3.

[12] Cic. *Att.* XIV. 20, 5.

[13] Cic. *Rep.* I. 3.

[14] Cic. *Rep.* I. 1, *id.* 4.

[15] Cic. *Rep.* I. 39.

[16] Cic. *Rep.* I. 45, *id.* 65, *id.* 68.

[17] Cic. *Rep.* I. 45, II. 45. Cf. III. 34, *id.* 41.

[18] Cic. *Rep.* II. 21.

[19] Cic. *Rep.* IV. 3.

[20] Cic. *Leg.* II. 35.

[21] Cic. *Leg.* II. 23, III. 12.

[22] Cic. *Rep.* IV. 3, *Leg.* III. 28–30. Cicero promises a further discussion of education, but this is missing in the *Laws* as we have it.

[23] Cic. *Rep.* IV. 6, *Leg.* III. 47.

[24] Cic. *Rep.* IV. *fin.*, *Leg.* II. 38–9, cf. III. 32.

[25] Cic. *Rep.* I. 54 f., II. 51.

[26] Cic. *Q.F.* III. 5, 1, *Rep.* VI. 8, *id.* 13.

[27] Cic. *Rep.* III. 33.

[28] Cic. *Leg.* I. 22 f.

[29] Cic. *Leg.* I. 28–31.

[30] Cic. *Leg.* I. 33.

[31] Cic. *Rep.* III. 20–1.

[32] Cic. *Rep.* III. 35–6.

[33] Cic. *Off.* II. 11, *id.* 21–8.

[34] Cic. *Off.* II. 73.

[35] Cic. *Off.* III. 28, II. 74.

[36] Cic. *Off.* I. 35.

[37] Cic. *Rep.* V. 1.

CHAPTER V (pages 54 to 65)

[1] See Cic. *Off.* III. 4.

[2] Cic. *Tusc.* I. 5–6, II. 6, *Div.* II. 5.

[3] Cic. *Div.* II. 4; cf. *Fin.* I. 10.

[4] Cic. *Div.* II. 6–7; cf. *Tusc.* I. 7.

[5] Cic. *Div.* II. 2, *N. D.* I. 10.

[6] Cic. *Fam.* XIII. 1, 2, *Brut.* 306.

[7] Respect for Plato: Cic. *Leg.* I. 15, II. 14, III. 1, *Pet. Cons.* 46, *Att.* IV. 16, 3, *Fam.* I. 9, 12, *id.* 18. Politics and literature: Cic. *Fin.* IV. 61, *Tusc.* II. 7.

[8] Cic. *Ac. Pr.* II. 7–8.

[9] Cic. *Tusc.* IV. 7, *Fin.* I. 15, *id.* 27; cf. *N. D.* I. 1, *Div.* II. 1, *id.* 28, *Tusc.* II. 4.

[10] Cic. *Tusc.* II. 5, V. 33.

[11] Cic. *N. D.* I. 6; cf. *Ac. Pr.* II. 11.

[12] Cic. *N. D.* III. 95.

[13] Cic. *Off.* II. 7–8.

[14] Cic. *Fin.* V. 79 f., *Tusc.* V. 22.

[15] Cic. *Tusc.* V. 83 f.

[16] Cic. *Hort.* fr. 42 Orelli.

[17] Cic. *Ac. Post.* I. 11.

[18] Cic. *Div.* II. 4.

[19] Cic. *Tusc.* V. 5.

[20] Cic. *Off.* I. 2.

[21] Cic. *Tusc.* II. 11, V. 19.

[22] Cic. *Tusc.* V. 3–5.

[23] Cic. *N. D.* III. 5 f.

[24] Cic. *Leg.* II. 32.

[25] Though Cicero attempts to bring Greek philosophy into line with Roman tradition by arguing that the old Roman rules about burial prove a belief in survival. *Tusc.* I. 27, *Lael.* 13.

[26] Cic. *Tusc.* I. 78, *id.* 60.

[27] Cic. *Tusc.* I. 79.

[28] Cic. *Rep.* VI. 26.

[29] Cic. *Tusc.* I. 66, *Cat. Maj.* 77. Cf. *Lael.* 13–4.

[30] Cic. *Cat. Maj.* 84.

[31] Cic. *Fin.* III. 7.

[32] Cic. *Parad. Proem.* 1–4.

[33] Cic. *De Or.* I. 56, *id.* 69, *Or.* 118.

[34] Cic. *Rep.* VI. 20–5.

[35] *ap.* Lact. *Inst. Div.* III. 14, 17.

[36] Cic. *Att.* XII. 52, 2.

[37] Plut. *Crass.* III. 3, *Pomp.* XLII. 5.

[38] Cic. *Fin.* I. 1–11, *N. D.* I. 6, *id.* 8, *Off.* II. 2.

[39] Plut. *Cat. Min.* LXVII (Perrin's translation).

[40] Plut. *Cat. Min.* LXVIII–LXXI.

CHAPTER VI (pages 66 to 77)

[1] Cic. *Div.* II. 5.

[2] Sen. *Suas.* VI. 1.

[3] Virg. *Aen.* XII. 818.

[4] Vitr. II. 1, 1 f.

[5] Vitr. II. 2, VIII. 3, IX. 1, *id.* 4.

[6] Prop. III. xxi. 25–6.

[7] Hor. *Sat.* II. iii, vii, *Odes* I. xxix. 13–14.

[8] Hor. *Sat.* I. v. 101, iii. 96 f.

[9] Ofellus's recommendation of plain living in *Sat.* II. ii is not necessarily Stoic, though we note the Stoic phrase *divinae particulum aurae* (79) and the surprising and very un-Epicurean recommendation to give money to restoring temples (104–5).

[10] Hor. *Sat.* II. iii.

[11] Hor. *Odes* I. xxxiv.

[12] II. ii. and III. xxix. (esp. 53 f.) are perhaps the most Stoic of the Odes.

[13] Hor. *Ep.* I. i. 16–19; cf. I. xvii. 23 f.

[14] Hor. *Ep.* I. i. 106 f.
[15] Hor. *Ep.* I. xvi. 73–9.
[16] *App. Verg. Cat.* V.
[17] Virg. *Georg.* II. 490.
[18] Virg. *Georg.* I. 415 f.
[19] Virg. *Georg.* IV. 219 f.
[20] Virg. *Georg.* I. 125 f.
[21] Virg. *Georg.* I. 133.
[22] Quint. VI. iii. 78.
[23] Compare Horace's words about Augustus:

> quo nihil maius meliusve terris
> fata donavere bonique divi
> nec dabunt. (*Odes* IV. ii. 37–9.)

The lines recall some words of Plato about philosophy (*Tim.* 47B), and in view of the frequent references in Cicero to Plato's words (*Ac. Post.* i. 7, *Leg.* I. 58, *Lael.* 47, *Tusc.* I. 64, *Off.* II. 5, *Fam.* XV. iv. 16) the reminiscence appears intentional.

[24] See Schanz-Hosius, *Geschichte der römischen literatur* III. pp. 163–4.
[25] Prop. III. v. 23 f., Virg. *Georg.* II. 475 f.
[26] Hor. *Ep.* I. ii. 29.
[27] Hor. *Sat.* I. iv. 26, i. 23–36, *Ep.* I. x. 30, *id.* 47. Avarice was recognized as the prevailing vice of Rome. See Seneca's remarks on the popularity of *sententiae* of Publilius Syrus on this theme. (*Ep.* cviii. 8.) Note also that Virgil makes the avaricious the *maxima turba* in Tartarus (*Aen.* VI. 611) and Vitruvius accounts it as the most important gift of philosophy to an architect that it makes him *sine avaritia* (I. 7).
[28] Hor. *Ep.* I. ii. 62, *id.* 32 f.
[29] Hor. *Ep.* I. xvii. 27 f., xviii. 5 f., xvii. 41–2.
[30] Hor. *Sat.* I. iii. 19.
[31] Hor. *Ep.* II. ii. 205 f.
[32] Sen. *Contr.* I. pref. 23. In a *controversia* about a vestal virgin who survived after being thrown from the Tarpeian rock the question was raised whether the gods care for human affairs; if so, whether for individuals, and in particular for the Vestal virgin. One rhetorician (Albucius) was blamed *quod haec non tanquam particulas incurrentes in quaestionem tractasset sed tanquam problemata philosophoumena. Contr.* I. 3, 8.
[33] Vegetarianism was 'in the air'. Sextius approved it, though not on Pythagorean grounds. Sen. *Ep.* cviii. 17 f.
[34] Ov. *Trist.* IV. x. 117–18.
[35] Sen. *Ep.* lix. 7, lxiv. 2–3.
[36] Plut. *Prof. Virt.* 77E, Suet. *Gram.* xviii.

CHAPTER VII (pages 78 to 88)
[1] Suet. *Aug.* 93.
[2] Hor. *Odes*, III. vi. 1–8. Cf. Prop. III. xxii. 21.
[3] Hor. *Sat.* II. ii. 103–5.
[4] Virg. *Aen.* I. 279.
[5] Virg. *Georg.* I. 24 f., cf. 503; *Aen.* I. 289–90.
[6] Hor. *Odes*, I. ii. 41 f., III. iii. 9 f., v. 2 f.

7 Virg. *Georg.* II. 472–3.
8 Lucr. IV. 590–2.
9 Virg. *Georg.* II. 493–4.
10 Virg. *Georg.* I. 343–50.
11 Hor. *Odes*, III. xxiii, xiii, xviii.
12 Tib. I. i. 11 f.; cf. I. v. 27 f.
13 Tib. II. i. 1–32.
14 Tib. II. i. 37.
15 Hor. *Odes*, I. xxxi, I. x, III. xxv, I. xviii, 11 f., II. xix.
16 Plat. *Phaed.* 61B.
17 Hor. *Sat.* I. iii. 99 f.
18 Hor. *Odes*, I. xvi. 13 (cf. Prop. III. v. 7, Ov. *Met.* I. 82 f.), I. x. 1 f.
19 Virg. *Georg.* I. 121 f.
20 Virg. *Aen.* VIII. 314 f.
21 Ov. *Am.* II. xiii. 7 f. It may be noted that she is attempting to procure an abortion.
22 Pers. I. 71–3.
23 Ov. *Ars Am.* I. 637 f.
24 Virg. *Georg.* I. 62.
25 Ov. *Met.* XV. 861 f.
26 Virg. *Georg.* I. 498 f.

CHAPTER VIII (pages 89 to 102)

1 Cic. *Ac. Post.* I. 9.
2 Cic. *De Or.* I. 193–6, *Fin.* I. 10, *Tusc.* I. 1.
3 Cic. *Fin.* I. 10.
4 Virg. *Ecl.* I. 3–4, 70–2.
5 Virg. *Georg.* II. 170 f.
6 Virg. *Georg.* II. 136 f.
7 Virg. *Georg.* II. 532–5.
8 Virg. *Georg.* II. 486 f.
9 Virg. *Aen.* I. 234 f.
10 Virg. *Aen.* IV. 231, VI. 781–2, VII. 99–100.
11 Virg. *Aen.* I. 286 f., VI. 791 f., VIII. 675 f.
12 Virg. *Aen.* VI. 847 f.
13 Virg. *Aen.* 836 f.; cf. I. 283–6.
14 Virg. *Aen.* XI. 336 f., I. 148 f.
15 Virg. *Aen.* VI. 826 f.
16 Virg. *Aen.* VIII. 670.
17 Tac. *Ann.* IV. 34, Sen. *Suas.* VI. 21.
18 Hor. *Odes*, I. xii. 35–6.
19 Hor. *Epod.* VII. XVI.
20 Hor. *Odes*, I. xxxvii.
21 Hor. *Odes*, I. xiv. 17–18.
22 Hor. *Odes*, III. xxix. 25–6.
23 Hor. *Odes*, I. ii. 21 f.; cf. I. xxxv. 29 f., III. vi. 13 f.
24 Hor. *Odes*, III. v. 10–11.
25 Hor. *Odes*, III. vi. 37–9.
26 Hor. *Odes*, III. ii. 1 f.
27 Prop. II. vii. 5–6, 13–14.

[28] Prop. III. iii, ix.

[29] Prop. III. xxii. 17–18, 21–2.

[30] Hor. *Odes*, III. vi. 17 f., xxiv. 21 f.

[31] Hor. *Odes*, III. xxiv. 25–9.

[32] Hor. *Odes*, IV. v. 21–2.

[33] Hor. *Odes*, IV. xv. 9 f.

[34] Arellius Fuscus *ap.* Sen. *Contr.* II. i. 18. Cf. Ov. *Fast.* I. 225. *laudamus veteres sed nostris utimur annis.*

[35] Extravagant building: Hor. *Odes*, II. xv, III. i. 33 f., Sen. *Contr.* II. i. 11–13, V. v. 1–2. Power of money: Prop. III. xiii. 48, Ov. *Fast.* I. 217–18, Sen. *Contr.* II. i. 7.

[36] Tac. *Dial.* 22,

[37] Vitr. II. viii. 17, Hor. *Odes*, III. xxiv. 9 f.

[38] Tac. *Ann.* III. 55. Seneca, however, considered that the young men of his day were less extravagant than those of Cicero's day. *Ep.* xcvii. 1–9.

[39] Sen. *Contr.* II. 7, 7.

[40] Hor. *Odes*, III. vi. 46–7, Liv. I. pref., Prop. III. xiii. 60.

[41] Tib. I. x. 29 f. Prop. III. v. 1, Ov. *Am.* III. ii. 49–50.

[42] Prop. III. v. 3 f., Tib. I. x. 7, II. iii. 35 f.; cf. Fabianus *ap.* Sen. *Contr.* II. i. 10 f.

[43] Hor. *Odes*, I. xxix.

[44] Hor. *Odes*, I. iii. 9 f., III. xxiv. 36 f., Prop. III. vii. 1, Tib. I. iii. 35–50, Ov. *Am.* II. xi, III. viii. 35 f.

CHAPTER IX (pages 103 to 114)

[1] Tac. *Ann.* IV. 33.

[2] Tac. *Hist.* I. 1.

[3] Sen. *Clem.* I. 1, 2, *id.* 4; I. 8, 5, *Cons. Pol.* VII. 2. Musonius, p. 36, 23 f. (Hense).

[4] Sen. *Clem.* I. 12, 1.

[5] Tac. *Dial.* 41. There is a revealing passage in Pliny's *Panegyricus* (3, 4), which suggests that praise of a ruler's virtues might really mean that he did not possess any such virtues.

[6] See Wirszubski, *Libertas as a Political Idea at Rome*, pp. 160–1.

[7] Tac. *Ann.* IV. 34–5.

[8] Luc. VII. 444–5.

[9] Luc. III. 145–6, Sen. *Clem.* I. 1, 7–8.

[10] Sen. *Ben.* II. 20, 2, *Const. Sap.* II. 2, *Ep.* XIV. 7–13.

[11] Luc. VII. 695–6, IX. 603.

[12] Sen. *Clem.* I. 1, 7–8, *id.* 4, 1–2.

[13] Sen. *Tranqu.* 1, 10.

[14] Sen. *Tranqu.* 3, 2.

[15] Sen. *Tranqu.* 1, 11.

[16] Sen. *De Otio*, 1, 4, *id.* 2, 1, *Ep.* viii. 1, lxviii. 10.

[17] Sen. *De Otio*, 3.

[18] Sen. *De Otio*, 4–6. *Ep.* lxviii. 1–2.

[19] Sen. *Ep.* viii. 1, *id.* 6, xxi. 2, lv. 4.

[20] Sen. *Ep.* viii. 7, xix. 6, xxxvii. 3.

[21] Sen. *Ep.* xxi. 1.

[22] Sen. *Ep.* lxxiii. 1–5.

[23] Sen. *Ep.* xiv. 7–13.
[24] Tac. *Ann.* XIV. 57, XVI. 22.
[25] Tac. *Hist.* IV. 5; cf. Dio, LXV. 12.
[26] Dio, LXV. 12, 2.
[27] Tac. *Hist.* IV. 5–6; cf. Wirszubski, *op. cit.* p. 149.
[28] Dio Chrys. περὶ βασιλείας III. 47.
[29] Epict. III. xiii. 9–11.
[30] Epict. IV. i. 1.
[31] Epict. I. xii. 9.
[32] Tac. *Agr.* 4.
[33] Tac. *Agr.* 4.
[34] Tac. *Ann.* XVI. 21, *Hist.* IV. 5.
[35] Tac. *Agr.* 42.
[36] Tac. *Ann.* IV. 20, 5.
[37] Tac. *Dial.* 40.
[38] Tac. *Dial.* 37–8.
[39] Tac. *Dial.* 41.
[40] Tac. *Hist.* I. 1.
[41] Tac. *Ann.* IV. 32–3.
[42] Tac. *Hist.* I. 1, *Ann.* I. 2.
[43] Tac. *Ann.* II. 88, *Agr.* 30.
[44] Tac. *Agr.* 21.
[45] Tac. *Hist.* IV. 74.
[46] Tac. *Agr.* 3; echoed by Plin. *Pan.* 36, 4.
[47] M. Ant. I. 14.
[48] M. Ant. VI. 12.
[49] M. Ant. VI. 44.
[50] Tert. *Apol.* 37.

CHAPTER X (pages 115 to 123)
[1] Tac. *Ann.* IV. 20, 5.
[2] Tac. *Ann.* VI. 22, Luc. II. 7 f., Plin. *N. H.* V. 22–3.
[3] Tac. *Ann.* VI. 22.
[4] Sen. *N. Q.* II. xlv.
[5] Sen. *Ben.* IV. vii.
[6] Epict. I. vi. 1–22.
[7] Epict. I. xvi. 1–18.
[8] Epict. I. vi. 23 f.
[9] Enn. *Scen.* 318 (Vahlen's 2nd edn.).
[10] Tac. *Ann.* VI. 22.
[11] Luc. VII. 445–7.
[12] Luc. II. 1, VII. 85–6, VIII. 70–1, 77, 486–7, 665, 763–4, IX. 186–8.
[13] Sen. *Prov.* 1, 5 to 2, 12, *id.* 4.
[14] Sen. *Prov.* 5–6, esp. 5, 8; cf. *Ben.* IV. 28 f.
[15] Sen. *Ep.* xcvi. 1–2, cvii. 11.
[16] Fronto, *De Nepote Amisso*, ii (Loeb edn. II, pp. 222 f.).
[17] Tac. *Agr.* 46.
[18] Lact. *Inst. Div.* I. 5, II. 8, VI. 24–5 (Sen. Frs. 16, 122, 24, 123).
[19] Sen. *Ep.* lxxiii. 12–14.
[20] Sen. *Ep.* xli. 3–4; cf. lix. 14. *Sapiens . . . cum dis ex pari vivit.*

[21] Luc. IX. 601–4.
[22] Epict. II. xix. 27, I. iii. 1.
[23] Aug. *C. D.* VI. 10 (Sen. Frs. 31–40).
[24] Sen. *Ep.* xxxi. 5.
[25] Sen. *N. Q.* II. xxxvii. 2, V. xxv. 4, *Ben.* V. xxv.
[26] Sen. *Ep.* xcv. 47–50, xli. 1 f, Fr. 123.
[27] M. Ant. IX. 40.
[28] Pers. II, Juv. X. 345 f.
[29] Tac. *Hist.* IV. 58, Plin. *Pan.* 94.
[30] Tac. *Hist.* III. 72, IV. 53.
[31] Plin. *Pan.* 1, 4, *id.* 8, 1.
[32] Fronto *Ad M.Caes,* V. 25 (Loeb edn. I, p. 212), *Ad Ant. Pium.* 5 (Loeb edn. I, p. 228), *Ad Verum Imp.* ii. 6 (Loeb edn. II, pp. 84–6), **Brock,** *Studies in Fronto and his Age,* pp. 87 f.
[33] *Hist. Aug. M. Ant.* iv. 2–4, xiii. 1–2.
[34] M. Ant. V. 33, VI. 30.
[35] M. Ant. IV. 27.
[36] M. Ant. II. 13, III. 6, 7, 16.
[37] M. Ant. IV. 23.
[38] Min. Fel. *Oct.* vi. Cf. Symmachus, *Relationes,* III (Seeck's edn., p. 282): *iam si longa aetas auctoritatem religionibus faciat, servanda est tot saeculis fides et sequendi sunt nobis parentes, qui secuti sunt feliciter suos.*

CHAPTER XI (pages 124 to 134)
[1] M. Ant. X. 16. Much the same was said by the Christian Lactantius. *Non studendum sapientiae . . . sed sapiendum est. Inst. Div.* III. 16.
[2] Sen. *Ep.* lxxx. 4, lxxxi. 13. See Pohlenz, *Die Stoa,* I, p. 319.
[3] Sen. *Ep.* cviii. 3, *id.* 14, *id.* 22.
[4] Pers. V. 41–4.
[5] *Hist. Aug. M. Ant.* III. 5.
[6] Sen. *Ep.* lii. 2, *id.* 8.
[7] Sen. *Ep.* xxv. 6; cf. xi. 9–10.
[8] Sen. *De Ira,* III. 36.
[9] Sen. *De Ira,* II. 20, III. 8–9.
[10] Epict. II. xviii. 12–13.
[11] Sen. *Ben.* I. 4, 1, *Ep.* lxxxiii. 9.
[12] Sen. *Const. Sap.* 3.
[13] Sen. *Const. Sap. passim.*
[14] Sen. *De Ira,* I. 12, 1, II. 13, 3, *id.* 16, 1.
[15] Sen. *Clem.* II. 6.
[16] Sen. *Cons. Helv.* 9–12, *Tranqu.* 8–9, *Ep.* iv. 11, xx. 6 f., cx. 12 f., cxix. 5.
[17] See Sen. *Brev.* 12–13.
[18] Sen. *Tranqu.* 2.
[19] Sen. *Const. Sap.* 1, *Prov.* 3, *Ep.* lxvii. 14, lxiv. 4–5.
[20] Sen. *Ep.* xviii. 7.
[21] Sen. *Ep.* lxxvii. 6.
[22] Sen. *Ep.* xxiv. 35–6.
[23] Sen. *Clem.* II. 5–6.
[24] Sen. *Ep.* xlvii. 1; cf. *Ben.* III. 22.
[25] Sen. *Clem.* I. xviii.

²⁶ Sen. *Ep.* xlvii. 11.

²⁷ Sen. *Ep.* vii.

²⁸ Sen. *De Ira*, II. 7–8.

²⁹ Sen. *Ep.* vii.; cf. x. 1, *Vit. Beat.* 1–2.

³⁰ Sen. *Cons. Marc.* 20. Pliny the elder considers it to be the chief consolation for man's imperfect nature that God cannot do everything; for example, 'he cannot, even if he wished, commit suicide, the best gift he has bestowed on man among the great ills of life'. *N. H.* II. 27.

³¹ Aug. *Civ. Dei*, XIX. iv. 4.

³² Sen. *Ep.* lxx. 14–15.

³³ Sen. *Ep.* lxx. 18.

³⁴ Mus. VIII (p. 38 Hense), XVI. (p. 87 Hense).

³⁵ Mus. III-IV (pp. 8–19 Hense).

³⁶ Mus. XII-XV (pp. 63–81 Hense). Compare Epictetus's remarks about bathing the baby, etc. (III. xxii. 67 f.). He is discussing whether the Cynic should marry, and decides against. He regards Crates's marriage as an exception. Musonius, on the other hand, quotes the case of Crates to prove his point.

³⁷ Mus. XI. (pp. 54–63 Hense).

³⁸ Epict. I. i. 14–25, xviii. 17, IV. i. 81 f.

³⁹ Epict. III. iii. 14 f., I. xii. 17 f.

⁴⁰ M. Ant. II. 16; cf. II. 1, V. 33.

⁴¹ M. Ant. VII. 31.

⁴² M. Ant. V. 10, II. 1, IX. 3.

⁴³ Aug. *Ep.* CXVIII. 21.

⁴⁴ Quint. XII. ii. 30.

CHAPTER XII (pages 135 to 145)

¹ Gell. XIII. 17.

² Cic. *Fam.* III. 2, 1, *Att.* I. 17, 4. See Schneidewin, *Antike Humanität*, Reitzenstein, *Werden und Wesen der Humanität im Altertum.*

³ Cic. *Q. F.* I. 1, 25, *id.* 21; cf. *Fam.* XIII. 65, 1.

⁴ Cic. *De Or.* I. 32.

⁵ Cic. *Caec.* 104, *Rab. Perd*, 26, *Balb*, 18, *Planc.* 58. See Pohlenz, *Die Stoa*, I, p. 274.

⁶ Cic. *Leg.* III. 1.

⁷ Cic. *De Or.* III. 48; cf. *Arch.* 4.

⁸ Cic. *De Or.* III. 94, II. 72, *Arch.* 3, *De Or.* II. 154.

⁹ Cic. *De Or.* II. 40, *id.* 153.

¹⁰ Cic. *Q.F.* I. 1, 7.

¹¹ Cic. *Q.F.* I. 1, 22.

¹² Ter. *Heaut.* 77.

¹³ Cic. *Off.* I. 134.

¹⁴ Cic. *Fam.* IX. 24, 3.

¹⁵ Cic. *Arch.* 1–4, *Att.* VII. 7, 7.

¹⁶ Cic. *Rep.* I. 29. Vitruvius attributes the saying to Aristippus (VI. *Proem.* 1).

¹⁷ Plin. *N. H.* III. 39.

¹⁸ Plin. *Ep.* VIII. 24, 2. The idea comes from Cic. *Q. F.* I. 1, 6. Cf. also Corn. Nep. *Att.* 3.

[19] Even the typically Roman ideal of *gravitas* combined with *humanitas* has its counterpart in Isocrates's advice to Nicocles to be ἀστεῖος καὶ σεμνός. *Ad Nic.* 33.

[20] Cic. *De Or.* I. 132, *Rep.* I. 36.
[21] Cic. *Fin.* V. 8, *N. D.* I. 56, *De Or.* II. 361.
[22] Cic. *De Fato.* 4.
[23] Cic. *De Or.* II. 17–18; cf. I. 221.
[24] *D. L.* VI. 73, 103–4.
[25] *D. L.* VI. 27–8.
[26] Cic. *Tusc.* IV. 69–71, II. 27, *Rep.* IV. 9.
[27] Cic. *Arch.* 16.
[28] Cic. *Att.* IV. 10, 11, *Fam.* IX. 1, 2, *Att.* IV. 8a; cf. *Att.* II. 6, 1, I. 20, 7.
[29] Cic. *Off.* I. 50, *id.* 94.
[30] Cic. *Tusc.* I. 6.
[31] Cic. *Tusc.* I. 7, II. 9, *Fat.* 3, *Off.* I. 2.
[32] *ap.* Lact. *Inst. Div.* III. 19, 6, I. 15, 20.
[33] Plin. *Ep.* VIII. xix. 1, II. iii. 8.
[34] Plin. *Ep.* VIII. xvi. 3, xxii, xxi. 1, V. iii. 2.
[35] Sen. *Ep.* lxxxviii.
[36] The Epicurean attitude was similar. Cic. *Fin.* I. 72.
[37] Sen. *Ep.* xc. 7 f.
[38] Epict. II. xvi. 33, IV. iv. 2, *id.* 36.
[39] Epict. II. xxiii. 23 f.
[40] M. Ant. I. 7, 2, II. 2, 3.
[41] M. Ant. IX. 36, XI. 2.
[42] Fronto, *Ad Amicos*, i. 2 (p. 174 Naber).

CHAPTER XIII (pages 146 to 152)
[1] Ambr. *Off. Min.* III. viii. 53, Lact. *Inst. Div.* IV. 10, 5.
[2] Min. Fel. *Oct.* 25; cf. Lact. *Inst. Div.* I. 18, 8–9, VI. 6, 19, II. 6, 12–13.
[3] Aug. *Civ. Dei.* I. xxx.
[4] Lact. *Inst. Div.* VII. 15, 11–17.
[5] Lact. *Inst. Div.* II. 6, 7–11.
[6] Min. Fel. *Oct.* 20.1.
[7] Lact. *Inst. Div.* II. 5, 37; cf. VII. 3, 3 f.
[8] Min. Fel. *Oct.* 38.6.
[9] Aug. *Contr. Ac.* III. xvii. 42.
[10] Pascal, *Sur Epictète et Montaigne.*
[11] See p. 59.
[12] Lact. *Inst. Div.* VI. 14 f.; cf. Aug. *Civ. Dei.* XIV. ix.
[13] Epict. II. xix. 27.

INDEX

170